READ
OR DIE

A story of survival, hope, and how
a life was saved one book at a time

DAPHNE RUSSELL

Published by Wheatmark®
2030 East Speedway Boulevard, Suite 106
Tucson, Arizona 85719 USA
www.wheatmark.com

ISBN: 978-1-62787-605-6 (paperback)
ISBN: 978-1-62787-606-3 (ebook)
LCCN: 2018940909

"The teacher, as we know, can confer upon the pupil no powers which are not already latent within him... his sole function is to assist in the awakening of slumbering faculties... what he imparts out of his own experience is a pillar of strength for the one wishing to penetrate through darkness to light."

—*Rudolf Steiner,* How to Know Higher Worlds

Read or Die has been created with fictional names to protect both the innocent and the guilty. Some characters are compilations of multiple people due to the fact it would be impossible for a reader to keep track of so many people in a teacher's day. The essence, however, is completely factual.

For Pop, the greatest teacher I've ever known

ROOM 111

During Abel Cazares's seventh-grade year, I knew him only by name.

When he walked into my eighth-grade reading class, he could have been any student in khaki shorts and blue polo shirt, the scent of Old Spice beginning to fade. But when he introduced himself, his boyish face and his delicately combed hair came into focus, his seventh-grade rap sheet on replay in my mind as I put my hand out to shake.

"I'm Abel," he said.

Despite his clean clothes and high-dollar shoes, his backpack lay flat on his back, the thought of carrying pencils, paper, and notebooks not within this boy's definition of school.

"What do you do in here?" he asked, looking around at the words on the walls, a Hemingway quote on the chalkboard in the back of the room, one by Louis L'Amour under the first, my interpretive version of the definition of intelligence on the chalkboard next to the other two:

Intelligence: The ability to acquire, consider, and apply new information.

"We read," I said.

He looked around some more and then back at me. "Ah, Ms.," he said. "No offense, but I don't read."

"Don't worry," I said as I waved my hand toward the rows behind him. "They didn't either."

That's when he noticed the other students, their heads down, books flat on the desks. The only sound in the room was Abel's side shuffle.

"I can read," he clarified. "I just don't."

"You'll fit right in," I said, but he was already exhausting me.

Abel Cazares arrived partway through school, partway through the week, and even partway through second period, and I didn't even know why he had changed schedules or who had initiated or approved the change. All I knew was, I didn't have the time or inclination to argue with him. So I told him he could pick something from my shelf or he could go to the library.

"I'll go to the library," he said.

So I let him go.

When he returned, I didn't ask him what book he checked out, nor did I bother to find out if he could read it. All I knew was I had spent every day since then looking at him lying sideways on his desk, a juvenile-sized fantasy book listless next to his head. A hibernating bear had more energy than this boy.

Today I look around the room and note everyone else. A month ago this particular class was more like the first hour of Black Friday, and now, fifteen minutes into class, everyone is back at home, absorbed in their Black Friday *gangas*.

I call Abel over and motion that he needs to bring his book. As he slides onto the stool next to my desk, he reassumes his state of lethargy, upper body heavy and loose, resting on one elbow, his head in the palm of his hand.

"You've been here a week," I say. "What's that book you're reading?"

"This," he says as he taps the book toward me with his free hand.

"*The Summer of the Unicorn*," I say. "Looks fascinating."

"Yep," he says.

I ask him if it's the book he still wants to read. He says it is. I ask him if he likes it; he says he does. I ask him why he picked it.

"It has a pretty purple unicorn," he says.

"And purple is your favorite?" I say.

"Maybe."

From our first encounter, it was obvious Abel was no real bad boy, his computer history void of anything beyond the typical public-school misdemeanor. But the reality at Mission Heights Middle School is that switchblades and Southside tattoos in old-school English are a rare sighting. Where I work the epidemic is written in invisible ink.

I print his grades and tell him to pick the paper up off the printer.

When he brings it back, I take a marker from my desk and write in bold, clear letters, "My name is Abel Cazares, and I have done everything I can to never graduate from high school. Please help me make my dreams come true." I write his name in bold print too, draw a line above his name, and slide it back over to him.

He smiles as he looks down like I've just given him a free pass to roam the hallways or leave campus for lunch or a hundred dollars to be spent on anything having nothing to do with school.

Then I see him read the words, see the words pass his eyelids and sink into his psyche. He turns to look at me. I hold out a pen.

"Seriously, you're never going to make it, so just sign," I say. He shakes his head.

"Oh, come on," I say. "This is your plan, right? You have straight Fs, you're doing nothing in class, just like last year, so just sign the paper. Make a statement. Be brave—I'm here to help." I hold the pen closer to him. I want to make it easy for him to give up, give in, let the wave of apathy carry his lifeless body out to sea, let the sharks turn his body into tasteless chum.

He shakes his head again.

In this moment I don't know Abel any better than I know the girl who bags my groceries or the man who delivers my mail, but the second he entered my room, he made me an accomplice to crimes he was destined to commit against the eighteen-year-old Abel, the one filling out minimum-wage job applications, picking up his food stamp card, or sporting an orange one-piece suit and living life in an eight-by-ten-foot cell.

I print his grades in six classes, each one a testament in favor of Abel's retention in eighth grade, each one a piece of evidence stating Abel will never wear a cap or gown.

"Okay, go pick up all the papers off that printer." I point again to the far wall.

He walks over, looks down, and pauses. I suppose this makes sense—the last time he walked over to the printer it didn't go so well—but he grabs the stack and comes back to the stool next to my desk.

I look at his face.

It's not that I didn't see him before, his black hair, his dark-brown eyes, or his long eyelashes. It's not that I didn't notice his lanky, not-quite-man, not-quite-boy body.

It's not that I couldn't pick him out of a lineup.

It's that I don't want him picked out of a lineup.

That's what makes me look past the slouched shoulders and slumber-walk, past the I-don't-care affect.

"Do you know you are five times more likely to drop out of school than any of your friends with passing grades?"

"I am?" he says.

"But I have a plan," I say. "It starts with these teachers—do you want to hear, or am I wasting my time?"

He nods his head this time, fully aware that now there will be no free pass to roam the hallways coming his way, no windfall of cash falling from the ceiling.

I tell him how to talk to each of his teachers—the one who will cuss at him, the one who will be mad, the one who is waiting for Abel to man up, and the one who will be sweet and let him hand in makeup work.

"If you don't decide what you're going to do with your life," I say, "someone is going to decide for you."

"Like you?"

"No," I assure him. Someone with far more villainous ideas than me will be happy to open the door for him to come back into Mission Heights for eighth grade, round two.

"Here," I say as I put a book in his hand. "I usually don't let boys read this until they've read a few others for me, but I need you to read this as soon as possible."

He looks down at the cover, a picture of the back of a boy's head covered in cornrows, the title, *Tyrell*, across the top. This is the book the boys can't put down. Tyrell is the first person they ever cared about who they've never met.

"But what about my unicorn?" he says.

I tell him I'll have someone return it to the library as I tap the cover of *Tyrell*. "You'll like it, I promise. I'm also not kidding—we have a deal?"

"I had a unicorn," Abel says as he picks himself up off his elbow and stands. "All right. I'll read it."

"You will read it, or I'm not going to help you move onto ninth grade," I say. "I'm going to—"

"I know, I know. Help me drop out—drive the hearse to my funeral—I got you."

This makes me laugh. "'Hearse to my funeral?' Clever," I say. "But seriously, ask some of the guys in here. They'll tell you how great this book is."

Abel looks at me. I know what I just said doesn't make any sense, but I know he'll read it. The first year I changed my teaching style from whole-class book sets to individualized reading, I gave *Tyrell* to one of my boys. The day after, he'd returned to class with a grin from here to Mexico. "Ms.," Hector whispered. "There's a blow job on page three."

"Oh, yeah," I said. "Sorry?"

And I was sorry. I immediately pictured his mom storming into the school screaming, "What did you give my son?"

I heard myself explaining, "But he's reading—"

I heard her rapid-fire rant in Spanish.

I saw myself updating my résumé.

"You want me to take it back?" I said.

"Oh, no," he said. "I just didn't know there were things like that in books."

Oh, yes, my boy, I wanted to say. There are hand jobs and blow jobs and so much more. But I didn't say that.

"You don't have to read it," I said. "We can find something more G-rated."

He held *Tyrell* to his chest like a little boy holds his blankie. "Nah, I'm good," he said, and he walked back to his seat.

This class, these books, they aren't about what the students will find. Every book I give, every lesson I teach, is about *who* they will find.

What Abel doesn't know is that this is my last year as a classroom teacher—twenty-nine years in a classroom coming to an end, and I'm going out books a-blazin'. If Abel isn't careful, I may just snatch *Tyrell* out of his hands. I'll wait, of course, until Tyrell is alone with his girlfriend. Then we'll see if Abel says, "No offense, Ms. I don't read."

I laugh. I would do that.

The kids in my classes have never read an entire book, and they can't relate to Harry Potter and his magic wand. Abel is twenty-eight days behind everyone else, and I need to get enough books inside him to get his lungs to work again, mend his shattered heart, and kick the shit out of apathy.

I look forward to the day I see yellow caution tape stretched around my students' neighborhoods, the chalk outline of apathy on the ground, crushed by the weight of a thousand books.

No educator, no real educator, likes the kid who escapes his consequences, and the eighth grade team is going to make sure Abel pays for his apathy unless he can turn it around, change his grades, change his attitude, and change his relationships with his teachers. But I don't have 180 days anymore.

He's only given me 152.

2

EDUCATIONAL DECISIONS

Visible from my school's marque, is the rooftop of the building on the University of Arizona's campus where I learned the complexities of research analysis. The College of Education, Ed, is a five-minute walk and a few hundred research studies away from my classroom door.

Ed said his research would help inform my instruction.

He said his research was valid and his findings were sound.

He said educators make fifteen hundred decisions a day.

Not only does this number seem substantially low, but this number also does not accurately represent the number of questions I must ask myself in order to reach one decision. Maria asks if she can use the restroom, and I find myself in a quandary.

Does she have a medical condition?

Will she come back?

Did she come back last time?

Does she have a boyfriend?

Does she have a girlfriend?

Has she gotten caught smoking in the bathroom?

Has she asked yet today?

Did she ask yesterday?

Is there a pattern?

Is she sick?

Is she meeting someone?

Does she have her phone?

Seriously, will she come back?

Do I even want her back?

Is there time for her to make it back?

I consider how complicated bathrooms are and then the bell rings for the end of class. "Sure, Maria, you can go now," I say.

"Thanks, Ms.," she says, but I don't think she means it.

I swing my door open and step into the hallway. My neighbor, Maggie, and I have hall duty between each and every passing period.

"God hates me," Maggie says as one of Mission Height's most notorious members slinks past us into her room.

"That's possible," I say. "That boy is definitely one more reason not to name your child Jesus."

I follow the boy through Maggie's doorway and lean into her room, taking note of the entire character concoction of her class.

"That's basically my sixth period last year. I was out here yelling at Jesus for grabbing his crotch for the second time, while three girls shoved another one of my girls into the closet."

This is how Maggie and I converse, in four-minute increments.

"What did you think of our emergency staff meeting?" she says.

"Where we were all accused of being child molesters? I loved it."

Our principal had announced to us this morning that Mission Unified School District doesn't want us in dark, locked rooms with students.

"I like how he said, 'This is just common sense, people,'" I say.

"And how we signed a paper pinky, swearing we won't molest anyone," she says.

"Gotta love Mission Unified."

When the bell ending passing period chimes, we don't bother saying good-bye; we both know we'll be back. We always come back.

Entering my room is a visual reminder that all districts have principals with tendencies to hover their red pens over check boxes marked: Student work is displayed.

They want rotating decorations coupled with monthly representatives of the "high" expectations of the school.

In the beginning of school, my students write their names in letters both bubble and cursive on twelve-by-eight pieces of construction paper, a sign for each student stating who is in here and why they are important. My walls are sprinkled with hearts and flowers and footballs, every color under the sun.

They only come down when school ends.

Except for the hall of famers, they stay up every year.

"Ms., whose is that?" says someone.

"Oh, that's Bianca. She was a group-home kid, and she took that poster home every night for two weeks."

"It's tight," someone says.

"I know her," says someone else. "We were in the home together."

Inside, the students are restless, still settling, still buzzing from their four minutes of kinetic friction in the hallway.

I yell, "Get out your books, people," because despite having silent reading in the first twenty minutes every single day, some of my students still require personal invitations.

"Check out the objective on the board," I add.

I sit down at my computer, keeping a vigilant eye on the students.

"Let's go, beautiful people," I say to my remaining empty-handed stragglers. "This isn't day one; you already know we're reading, so read."

After I take attendance, I get up to walk around my room. An educational expert came by once and commented on the configuration of my students' desks. "You know those are cemetery tombstones, right?"

"My cornfield rows?" I said.

"Those aren't cornfields. Those are cemetery plots where children's souls die a painful death of boredom." He turned and looked at me. "Don't you read educational research?"

"No, not really anymore," I said. "Typically, I'm just here with these people."

Junior was just one of the hundreds of men and women who spend their days giving feedback for a living, walking through strangers' classrooms for fifteen minutes with little check boxes to mark Observed, Not Observed, Not Applicable, and Inexplicable.

"Groups foster a sense of community and promote intellectual and social skills students need later in the work world," he said, still looking at me, still clearly disappointed in the lapse in my *Education Weekly* subscription. "It's all about communication—listening and learning."

I wanted to ask if he was keeping his current physician or changing to one of the doctors from the Group Project School of Medicine.

I have twenty-five students in one class reading twenty-five different books.

There are no group projects in Ms. Russell's room.

Books in hand everyone's head is in their own space, their own world. Reading is a solo sport. No one reads out loud in here unless they have something to share.

I look toward Abel. He is clearly locked in and focused on *Tyrell*—well past the blow job.

I laugh. It's too late to take it from him.

Ed says, "Treat each student individually."

The district says, "Differentiate."

Mr. Tombstone said, "Everyone count off one through four."

In my classes I have 125 different reading levels with varying speeds, effort, intensity, and desire. I differentiate all day long.

The district? They think we're all child molesters.

They have no idea the actual spectrum of our skill set.

Just this morning I hailed my coworker as the cockroach-killing queen of the universe—my desk, my metal cabinet, the wood cabinets, the countertop, and the printer are all reminders about the party that happens when the lights go down at Mission Heights.

Last week when I opened the printer to fix a paper jam, flashbacks of my childhood kitchen scattered across the inside of the printer.

"It's warm in there," said my colleague, the sixth-grade social studies teacher/superhero roach killer. "And they eat paper."

"Oh?" I said. "But that liquidy liqueur the district thinks is poison is like moonshine to these little jerks. Sure, it's strong, but it's not lethal. We need lethal. And by the way," I added, "You know too much about roaches."

I'd called her to my room because I'd heard she had the good stuff, the delicate drops of delicious poison for the centimeter-long visitors.

"This should do it," she said, after walking around my room with a syringe of illegal goop she bought off the internet. "You'll see little dead ones soon, the smaller the better. That means we're getting them before they have more babies."

Crack for roaches.

Teachers really are miracle workers.

As I head back to my seat to call over my first victim of the morning, the counselor walks into the room.

A boy follows behind.

I already know this boy is not like Abel; this is not an in-school change. The fact that this is a midquarter/midweek transfer means this was most likely an admin-initiated change of schools.

His dishwater-gray polo says his old school was a uniform school.

His disheveled hair says he does not participate in father/son barbershop dates.

Mr. Scott says, "Ms. Russell, this is Manny. He's coming to us by way of Wakefield Middle School."

I reach out to shake hands.

Manny hesitates first and looks around the room to see who's looking. Within a few seconds, he puts his hand out too, but he's awkward and uncomfortable. I make another mental note—one day I'll need to show him how to shake hands.

"Nice to meet you, Manny. Take an empty seat. I don't have a seating chart, so you can sit anywhere you want."

I thank Mr. Scott and head back to my chair, where I can watch Manny and his interactions with others. The childhood quotes of our mothers and fathers about water seeking its own level applies here. Manny will seek others like himself. The question is, who are his people?

Students like Manny, who come into a new school in the middle of everything have a tendency to leave schools later and, again, in the middle of everything.

I sit down at my computer to write my friendly cockroach killer a thank-you email, and then I pull up Manny's name on the district's intranet.

The public associates triage with emergency rooms, but teachers practice triage on the daily, and we don't have doctors or an OR, and sometimes we don't even have a nurse.

I need as much information about Manny as I can find.

When I looked up Abel's grades, I also looked up his attendance as far back as kindergarten. He was at one school for elementary, and he'd been at Mission Heights since sixth grade. His grades don't reflect it, but his attendance has always been good.

The boy may not make it through high school, but it won't be because he changed schools.

What I learn about Manny is that he has maintained a 0.0 GPA since sixth grade, so I look further back and find he had decent grades as well as decent attendance in fourth grade.

In fifth grade, however, it's obvious something happened. His average scores dropped below average, his acceptable behavior became unacceptable, and his attendance worsened from sporadic to almost nonexistent.

Since that time he has had seven out-of-school suspensions, including one for marijuana sales, another for bringing a knife to school. He has had ten in-school suspensions, including three without details, only the words, "blatant defiance," in the comments section. Defiance could mean anything from talking back to refusal to comply to walking out of a room.

I'll ask Manny why he moved when I call him over today, but first I will fill in the gaps of Manny's history with guesses that Manny probably had rice with butter for breakfast, there are probably twice as many people as there are beds in the apartment where he lives, his mother is probably getting her welfare check on Friday, and his dad is probably not getting out of prison until Manny graduates, or doesn't.

I'm not sure how many days I have with Manny, but it's not 140.

I choose the book he's going to read based on facts and speculation. I don't have time to see if he can read on grade level, and I cannot use a state reading test to know what Manny knows. Sure, if he received a passing grade then he definitely can read, but the converse is not true.

What is apparent is that Manny hasn't been successful in school in a long time, and he needs to feel success *stat*.

For the record this does not mean when someone gets around to telling me more about him or when his file finally finds our school or when his old counselor calls Mr. Scott and tells him what he knows about Manny and then when Mr. Scott finally gets a minute to catch me up with all he learned.

No. I don't have that much time.

I treat Manny like books are EpiPens and he has a shellfish allergy and a mouth full of shrimp.

3

PROFESSIONAL DEVELOPMENT

After the last US school tragedy, our principal was instructed to leave only one entry access to the campus. At this door a camera and buzzer system alert our head secretary to see guests before they are allowed into the building.

He told us this security plan in the library, where our professional development takes place. "Development" is a misnomer, though. It's really just a staff meeting or lecture series or menial tasks afternoon, the idea of actual development far too complex for Mission Unified to comprehend. The juxtaposition of the walls of books quite the contrast to what actually happens in the library on Wednesday afternoons.

When he told us about the safety changes, the entire PE department raised their hands. "How are we supposed to get our kids to and from the field?"

"I'll make sure you all have keys to the gate," he said.

"We have to unlock the gate, cross the street, play, and come back and unlock it again?" they said.

"Yes," he said.

"What about passing period? Do we lock it and unlock it for those four minutes?"

The gate to the field is off a main street and nowhere near the school parking lot. Typically, it's wide open.

After a ten-minute discussion, it was decided our campus would be penetrable four minutes of every hour seven times a day.

The new safety procedures reinforce what Maggie and I do anyway, but we've become more diligent. In the past I would let people walk by without badges or IDs, but now we try to stop everyone, which usually means we meet the guys replacing the A/C filters or the women updating the computer software or the plumbers replacing the sink that was ripped off the wall.

Invariably the strangers in our hallway are district employees with badges we haven't seen at first glance.

Then today I get a stranger with no badge and no ID.

He is obviously both lost and terrified, huddled up next to the wall across from me, a death grip on his briefcase, and his other hand clenched into a fist.

He's wearing a pink pin-stripe shirt, black slacks, and shiny shoes. Even if he had a tie, it would still be evident he's no substitute. On any given day, substitutes don't know if they are watching an art class or a PE class or advanced tuba; they need comfortable shoes they can afford on an eleven-dollar-an-hour salary, not some freshly polished Cole Haans from Neiman Marcus.

Based on his inability to navigate middle school passing period, I decide the guy must be a life insurance salesman looking for the teachers' lounge. It's not unusual for these guys to troll our eating space, looking for new teachers eager to invest money in something in addition to our teacher retirement.

They buy three-foot long subs from the local grocery store and tempt new teachers with zesty Italian dressing and promises of high interest rates and higher yields.

I have to help him, but I don't really want to help him. I want to say, "Hey, buddy, if you can't walk through a middle school hallway like a big boy, then you don't deserve a teacher's trust."

Instead I approach him slowly, my hands behind my back in gentle recognition of his fragile situation. I lean down to eye level and say, "Can I help you?"

He grips the handle on his case harder and says something unintelligible.

I lean closer, trying not to scare this little mouse more.

"Excuse me?" I say.

This time I hear him. "I am C. S. Sandoval," he says.

His face suddenly registers. I've seen his picture in the newspaper and, more often than not, the front page of the district's intranet website.

"Oh!" I say. "You must be looking for the office—let me grab a student for you."

"That gate is wide open," says Dr. Sandoval. "Anyone could get in here."

Clearly, he's angry, disgusted, and appalled at our lack of security that allowed this well-dressed stranger to walk right into this hallway.

"Yes, I understand what you are saying," I say again. "Let me find you a student to take you to the office so you can talk to our principal about the gate."

I turn and happen to see Destiny behind me.

"Destiny!" I say. "This is Dr. Sandoval. Dr. Sandoval, this is Destiny."

I pull her close and let Dr. Sandoval make his own danger assessment of this teenager.

One of the tamest of the bunch, I want to tell him. She'll bring you homemade tamales at Thanksgiving and a pumpkin roll at Christmas. She'll draw adorable tiny hearts instead of dotting her i's, and she'll doodle extra hearts in the margins on every single assignment. She'll make you love her when she's in class and miss her when she's absent because she's one you can count on to make sure you're okay.

"I'll have her take you up to the office to meet our principal." Her smile seems to soothe him.

"Thank you," he says to me.

"Come on, Dr. Sandoval," says Destiny. "I'll show you where to go."

Just a few feet away are the double doors leading toward our administration offices. Destiny walks over and holds the door open for our distinguished guest, and she follows him for a moment and then gets ahead again to lead him. From this distance he looks more comfortable, his free hand no longer clenched.

To be fair, I'm certain the superintendent of Arizona's second largest school district isn't afraid of all children, just the ones he doesn't know.

The superintendent versus Manny, I know who would win.

What would the good doctor even do when Manny and Abel arrive minutes after the last bell? Let them go? Make them suffer?

It's Manny's second day, second period of school, and his first period is next door.

In layman's terms, one second tardy is hugging a few extra girls, hugging one girl longer, high-fivin' one more dude, knuckle bumping one more friend.

One minute late is a bathroom boy fest with body boxing and banter, and at Mission Heights, the potential for pot smoking is high.

As they walk into the room, Abel looks at me and says, "Sorry, Ms."

Manny avoids eye contact and heads straight for the back row.

He's lucky. I was about to attack, but Abel said the magic words, the words that take a lioness, jaws stretched in anticipation of dinner, and turn her into a lamb, cozy by the fire, warming her wool.

I am disappointed.

My *Men and Bathrooms* lecture is one of my favorites. I love helping young men be their best man-selves, my voice dangerously sarcastic as I harass them. "Ask 'em, ask your *tata* if he goes to the bathroom with other guys. Ask your *tio*. I can't wait to hear what they say."

I laugh, but it's not funny. My time with Manny has an elusive ending.

"Manny, come here," I say, already moving on, already in teacher mode, already ready to get this guy moving in the direction of school, one class at a time.

When he's close enough, I point to the stool next to my desk. "Sit," I say.

I slide a book called *The Bully* across my desk toward him.

He knows he's late. He knows I'm mad. He just doesn't know what I'm going to do about it.

I start with students on a stool higher than my office chair. It gives them the power they need to hear me without running, to listen without losing their manhood.

From the stiffness of his movements, I know he lacks the air of confidence needed to be a truly dangerous teenager.

"First of all, don't come late to my class. Second of all, if you do, then just look at me and say you're sorry, just like Abel did."

He starts to talk about needing the restroom, and I stop him.

"I don't want to hear any excuses. Just come on time or say you're sorry, and if you need the restroom, go with a pass after the bell rings." I pause. "But that's not why I called you over. I called you here to tell you we read. Everyone in here reads."

"But I don't like to read," he says.

I sweep my hand across the room, pointing out all the kids now reading silently. "Neither did they. Neither did your friend Abel." I point specifically to Abel. He's already pulling out his book, already finding his page. I make sure Manny sees what I see.

"What we do that no one probably told you is that you have to make connections to every single sentence."

"We have to think while we're reading?" he says. "That's whacked."

I laugh. "No one has ever called it 'whacked.' The books, maybe, but not thinking. But yes, you think constantly, and when you find yourself not making connections, stop reading, back up, read it again."

I tell him to open the book to page one and ask him to read.

"Out loud?"

"No, just to yourself, but think about your life as you read. Where does the character live? Where do you live? Who does he live with? Who do you live with? Those connections help you remember what you're reading."

Those connections are invaluable, I don't say. They make you turn the page, read to the end, read again, and continue reading when I'm not here begging.

I watch his face while he reads. I'm looking for understanding or skimming, fake reading or remembering, and when he finishes I pray he can answer my question.

"What's going on?" I say.

"He's starting at a new school."

"That's perfect. You just started here."

"Yeah," he says.

"How does he feel being new?"

"Scared, I guess."

"It is weird, isn't it? I've never been new, but I always made sure I talked to the new kids."

"I've always been the new kid."

"Well then, you and he have something in common, and you continue reading to see when those things are the same, and even if they are different, you still compare. I don't have to be a fifteen-year-old boy from Chicago to understand a fifteen-year-old boy from Chicago. Understand?"

He looks at me and nods his head.

Except for our introduction, this is the closest we've been.

My chair, that stool, our inaudible conversation...it's all a trap. I invite Manny to my house instead of going to his. I have nothing to hide: white hair, wrinkles, a face that says I've walked miles down these hallways. If he looked closely, he could see there's a sadness there too, eyes that say I'm almost done.

I am not Teacher of the Year material, and I let him know it's no secret. I have a history of imperfection.

I stare back at him, of course. I compare him to the three thousand students in my teacher Rolodex: fifteen hundred boys, fifteen hundred girls, of varying abilities, thoughts, ideas, dreams, aspirations, successes, and failures.

We're sizing each other up, no differently than wild animals, Manny and I. We are cops and robbers, rivals and allies.

I need to know the extent of the injury done to this boy, what caused the damage and how fourteen years of history will affect his future here with me.

I've had many students with parents in jail, many students who wear the same shirt they wore yesterday, the same shorts with the same stains day after day. They are poorly fed and scarcely loved, but they have potential.

My job is to find out just how much school potential Manny has. After today I will not ruminate on what he has done, but instead I will find out what he can do.

"Okay," I say, our time for assessment over. "Go read chapter one, and when you finish, whether that's today or tomorrow, come over with your book, and I'll test you on that chapter."

"Like just now?"

"Yep, only I'll read one sentence from the chapter, and you'll have to tell me what happened in that moment."

"All right," he says as he gets up and walks toward his desk.

I look at the clock. My time with Manny was ten minutes of my allotted fifteen minutes of silent reading, but I need to get to Abel.

If I ever were to go back to see Ed, visit and chat about what I learned since the last time we spoke, I would tell him he needs to investigate the significance of peer influence, possibly teach a class on how to change the classroom climate one peer at a time.

But he wouldn't understand. He thinks the teacher has such great influence over children. He's wrong. We have influence over a few children, and if we're smart, we empower the students who are achieving to seduce the others into achieving too.

When I call Abel over, I'm going to ask him questions he can answer and prove he's smarter than he thinks and more capable than he knows, and this conversation won't be as quiet as the one I had just now with Manny, making sure he knows the only attention students get in here is for school success.

I try to picture Sandoval meeting Manny, no more in common than similarly colored hair. Manny would make Sandoval twitch, Destiny more to his liking—her calm, sweet cleanliness soothing to his psyche.

An hour later I'm still reenacting my meeting with Sandoval, the storytelling aspect too titillating not to tell. When my audience finds out who snuck through our school security, they laugh uncomfortably. They're all teachers, of course.

The only nonteacher stopped me halfway through my delivery and put her hand on my arm soothingly. "It's the superintendent, isn't it?"

From that moment my story has not been as funny as it had been, the state of our campus security diminishing with every retelling, and to add to the reality, while Maggie and I share our last four-minute passing period of the day, we seem to sniff the air at the same time.

"Axe," she says.

I sniff again. "To hide the marijuana," I say. "I'll tell Mark."

The boys' bathroom is ten steps from my room and ten more to Mark's office, where the disciplinarian of my dreams houses the lunch detention and after-school detention students as well as the super naughty ones who need a full day or many days quarantined away from everyone else.

The part-time fighters, fire-alarm pullers, thieves, and mischief-makers are all part of his daily dealings. I open his door and catch his attention. "Somebody's being stupid in the boys' bathroom."

"On my way," he says, and he is; no walking for this guy. I've been trying to get the kids to call him Mark the Bounty Hunter.

"Why?" he asked one day, when I was bragging on his skills with changing kids' attitudes.

"Dude. You won't let a kid get away with anything."

"That's only because the kids think they can get out of detentions," he said.

"Right, and if they ditch detention, you give them another detention, and they think that's it, but it's not."

"Well, they still have to serve that first detention," he said matter-of-factly. "That's what everyone does ... don't they?"

Um, no, that's not what everyone does.

But when Mark heads to a drug bust, you can be sure he will catch the culprit, make them confess before he gets them to the office, and find out all the other guilty parties within the hour.

Then he might take a lunch break.

Or not.

"Tell me later about the Sandoval meeting," he says as he runs by. "I hear it was awesome."

"It'll be better over drinks," I say as he goes in for his drug bust and I enter my room for my final class of the day—thirty eighth graders, much like Abel's class of nonreaders and can't-readers all getting ready to read.

Although it will take a few minutes for them to settle, the scent of marijuana and Axe in the air is as much a deterrent to classroom order as a fight or fire alarm. I'm patient but insistent…books on desks…open books on desks…read books on desks.

"Let's go, people."

But the kids aren't the only ones distracted by the bathroom bust. I have no jurisdiction there, no say in what happens to whoever was in there doing whatever they did, but the lack of participation in that part of school sets no limitation on how I feel.

Was it Abel?

If so, who was he with?

How will it affect my classes?

Was it Manny?

Dammit.

Fear prevents me from moving forward, a history of students at my mind's tip, teacher melancholy a driving force at night when we have the least amount of control, naked-teaching nightmares consuming our sleep, late nights Facebook hunting former students.

Last week I looked one up because of Abel, his face a constant reminder I need to do more to set him free from his own melancholy chains.

Sabrina Clardy, my second-grade class of 1993, San Xavier Mission Elementary.

From her pictures I could see she has two kids and her mother is still alive and in her life.

It was really her, really Sabrina Clardy.

Three weeks ago I heard Mariachi music at a funeral and thought of an ex-student named Robert. I couldn't remember his last name, and I didn't know how to find him, but I still wondered where he was, how he was doing and what was he doing, and I was curious if he was still playing the viola.

I got a chance to ask him because he's the new receptionist at my bank.

The tie between student and teacher is not one of symbiosis, but meeting later, twenty-four years later, is also much more than serendipity.

We get 180 days with a child, give or take our own days off for the dentist, the chiropractor, a funeral, our monthly plasma donation.

If we have our own children, who knows how many days we'll miss: five days for a tonsillectomy, two days for the flu, one for a cold, half-day for the dentist too because little pookie had a cavity.

But the ties are still there, created on the days we are at school, with invisible strings society cannot see, the district ignores, and the state cannot measure.

I wonder what happened to so many of my kids.

Is Kyle in jail?

Is Celeste in jail?

Joelle is in jail? How did that happen?

I was positive Pedro was in jail, but then he bussed my table last week at Little Mexico.

And what about Fabian and Jocelyn and Sandy and Jimmy and Jason and Janae and Julissa? What about Jaime and Henry and Nicki? Did they graduate from high school? From college?

And Nico who used to be Nica?

Where are they all now?

What are they doing?

How are they doing?

Countless numbers of children in twenty-nine years, I can't remember them all, but there's no way I can forget them all.

Sabrina was embedded in me by her smile and her laugh and the deep resonance of her Ford 350 voice in her tiny Datsun body.

"Ms.," she'd say. "What's your favorite flower?"

I'd say, "Sunflower," and she'd draw me something more like a rose and less like anything I ever requested. I'd pin it up on the blackboard, and we'd stand back and smile.

I'd reach out and touch the corner of the paper. "You're a good artist," I'd say.

She'd say, "I know," then I'd feel little tiny fingers crawling into my hand, a quick squeeze before she'd run back to her desk, where she'd draw another roselike sunflower.

If it had rained and we were outside for recess, she would ask me about my favorite food. I'd look around, act as if I was in complete concentration over the all-important question, and I'd say something, always something different: enchiladas, scrambled eggs, French toast.

Then I'd look down at Sabrina's mud-caked, wrist-deep hands, and she'd slap together the dirtiest handful of grass, twigs, leaves, and mud and hold it out like she'd just gotten it off the stove, out of the oven, off the grill from her own special kitchen.

Her big smile would envelope her entire face, scrunching up her dark-brown eyes, wrinkling her temples.

"Here you go," she'd say, confident in her chef hands, chef heart, chef mind, her brown gooey patty.

With as much restraint as I could muster, I would reach down to take that blob of muck from Sabrina's tiny hands, delicately of course, as not to soil my own hand or my clothes, but with great gusto I would take a massive pretend bite and rub my belly with delight as if Sabrina's mud-packed burger blob was the very food I needed that day.

I would do anything to hear Sabrina laugh.

"You are the enchilada-making queen of the universe," I'd say, or New York strip-making, or Cornish Game Hen–making or dill pickle–making queen of everything.

"Aw, Ms. You're so funny when you're playin'," she'd say back, and then she'd just keep on laughing until it was time to go inside and wash up for whatever thrilling lesson I was going to teach next.

No, I didn't teach her how to read.

I didn't teach her the times tables or science or social studies or anything academically improving.

If I did, it was an accident.

I was a third-year teacher on my third grade. I had yet to get my feet settled into one curriculum. The best I could do was paint a new Jackson Pollock painting a day with ideas and thoughts, topics and lessons all over the place. A smattering of reading here, a smidge of math there, a splash of Rosa Parks and a sprinkle of volcanoes and Egyptian history all held together for years without me looking too much like an incompetent nincompoop.

Sabrina learned despite me.

I didn't need to discipline her or correct her or buy her new shirts or new shoes. I didn't need to mend her broken jacket zipper or feed her oranges in the morning or burritos in the afternoon. We didn't deliver food baskets to her house at Christmas, and I never had to send home a note saying, "Sabrina needs to improve her behavior."

Although, I wish I would have sent home a note that said, "Your daughter is amazing!" but I don't remember if I did.

What I do remember, what I know for a fact is, what Sabrina needed, what Sabrina demanded, what I had spent the first three years refusing to give up, was one in the same.

To be fair, she gave it to me first. I only had to return the favor.

Kids can be like that.

Damn kids.

All sticky-fingered, stain-shirted, tousle-haired, and snuggly.

Sabrina was like that.

The worst.

And don't slight me if I was rough around my blackboard edges.

I thought I had to be.

You don't understand.

There are a lot of kids in a classroom. That's a lot of love for one person to give and take away, and even today, twenty-nine years later, after checking my Facebook, I still have to work with other kids, new kids, kids who are six years away from me even thinking about accepting them as Facebook friends. I can't sit here and think about the kids who made me human.

"Ms. Russell," said Sabrina. "Why'd you want to become a teacher?"

"To hang out with kids like you," I said.

"Nah, really? Why? Didn't you want to be a doctor or lawyer or something fancy?"

"Fancy? And get paid more? No, jobs like that never crossed my mind. I just wanted to spend my day with kids like you and get paid for it. I make enough."

"Don't you want to make more?"

"Not if it means working with adults. I don't really like adults."

"Aw, Ms. Russell, now you're just playin' with me."

"No, no, I'm serious, Sabrina. You're the reason I'm a teacher."

I couldn't say what I wanted to; I was holding out, keeping on my side of the chalk-drawn line, but she didn't honor the line I'd drawn.

"Aw, Ms. Russell, I know you're kidding with me, but I'm glad you're a teacher—you're funny, you're smart, and you're good at four square, but I don't like you, Ms. Russell."

"What? You don't?" I said. I knew where this was going, but I didn't want to hear it.

She put her arms around my waist like she was consoling me.

"No, Ms. Russell," she said. "I don't like you. I love you."

Damn snuggly kids.

"I love you too, Sabrina."

Twenty-four years later I still love Sabrina. She opened the gates to the Mannys and the Abels and the Hectors of the world.

Sometimes I joke with the morning custodian. "Dude, seriously. Do you have to leave the gates open? Can't you keep 'em locked?"

"And not let the kids in?" he says, and laughs, our stand-up routine to rival Laurel and Hardy. "Sure, how 'bout tomorrow. You get it okayed with Pacheco."

We're kidding of course. The kids are the best part of the day, just not today.

Before I'm walking to today's professional development, Mark stops me in the hallway. He looks around to make sure no kids are listening. "Did you hear?"

"Nope," I say, and I don't really want to hear, but I must. I need to know how many bottles of wine to pick up for the rest of the week. It's only Wednesday.

"It's that new kid, Manny," he says. "And I think you have the other kid too—"

"Abel," I say, but it's not a question.

I'll need an entire bottle tonight. I may even start when I get home, no need to wait for dinner. I laugh; maybe I'll just have wine for dinner.

"Yeah, that's it," he says. "I guess one of them brought some weed to school."

Manny.

Of course they did.

At the end of the day, I read an email requesting homework for Manny.

Seventh period is over, but el jefe said the work needed to be dropped off by seventh.

There's no mention of Abel.

I make some copies at the office and hand multiple days' worth of work into the appropriate basket, but no one ever does the work put in there.

And I mean no one.

Not even the kids who are just sick.

It's required by law for teachers to provide work for those students put on suspension or those missing school for surgery or vacation or a dental cleaning, but students never do the work, and the copies for no one make me late to our professional development.

From the weekly announcements, I know we have a guest speaker from the University of Arizona's College of Counseling. She's an expert on cultural diversity.

I walk into the library just as she asks us how we define "culture."

From the back of the room, I yell, "Why ask us what culture is? Can't you just tell us, or do you have no idea?"

Not really. I don't say a thing. It's just that I know she doesn't understand what a culture of apathy is or a culture of peer pressure or a family culture of marijuana sales.

I take a seat and begin texting lots of inappropriate sexy male pictures with my friends.

"Check out this guy's huge tattoos," I text, with a picture I find off a high school friend's Facebook.

It's important to like your work environment and get along with coworkers. Exchanging R-rated pictures of spandex-wearing guys with six-pack abs makes all of us happy and alleviates much of the emotional pain and stress involved in worrying about drug-dealing students or listening to someone talk about something they clearly don't understand.

"He doesn't have tattoos," texts Maggie.

"I know," I reply.

It will take a second, but Maggie's entire table will bust out laughing when they see both of those texts.

Meanwhile the diversity trainer says we must be our "authentic selves."

I write, "'Be authentic,' says the lady with the tie-dyed hair," to all my R-rated pic buddies.

Then she talks about food and traditions and certain cultures: "… especially Native Americans," not liking, "… eye contact."

She's not taking questions or comments at this point, so I make a mental note to tell her later that I used to work on the Tohono O'odham Reservation sixty miles south of Tucson. On one occasion I drove a boy home for throwing rocks at his classmates for the second day in a row.

Even though I'd met Donovan's mother at open house just months before the flying rocks, when I arrived on Ms. Sixkiller's doorstep, I prepared myself for all the cultural norms people like Ms. Authentic-Self say exist. Ed told us about them too, of course.

Ed said, "Native Americans don't like to have their picture taken."

"Native Americans are quiet."

"They prefer to listen than to speak."

And my personal favorite, Native Americans respect the unique individual differences among people...

Ed tells us to differentiate and then dumps all Native Americans into one tribe.

Perhaps I should have referred Mrs. Sixkiller to Ed's handbook when she looked me in the eye and said, "The old people tell us not to let the white people in, but I trust you," then swung the door open so I could enter the house with little Donovan.

The boy sat and sulked in the corner while his mother and I talked just like regular teachers and parents talk. We chatted for at least an half hour about Donovan's potential, his brilliance, and his leadership qualities.

When all was said and done, that was his last rock.

Maybe I should have written Ed a letter and let him know Donovan's mother and I both spoke the same language—school.

He'd probably just say something else about "Native Americans."

I don't believe a child must be successful in school to be successful in life, but I do believe being successful in school is an indicator of being able to complete something. And when parents take an interest in school and their children's success in school, it makes my job easier.

I send a few more naughty texts to my pals in order to cleanse my mental palate of the diversity trainer's narrow-mindedness. I ask for wine suggestions too, of course.

After the meeting I hang out in my room awhile, straightening out my desk.

I check my email before I leave.

Still no news on Abel, but I won't be surprised by the outcome.

I don't think his family speaks school.

Manny's definitely don't.

4

CONTROL ISSUES

I learned about teacher mailboxes the semester I student taught, checking our mentor's mailbox part of our initiation, training, hazing...

"Check them before school, during your lunch, and before leaving for the day," they said.

I wanted to know why little Johnny couldn't check for mail, our best selves' best interest in the students. Johnny loves to run errands. Why can't Johnny run this errand?

"Because sending little Johnny is a FERPA violation, and we don't feel like going to jail," they said. "There could be classified documents in those boxes."

FERPA, the government-encrypted acronym telling us who to tell and who not to tell information about a student.

The mailman?

No.

A stranger at the gym?

Of course not.

The seven teachers who have the depressed student, the almost completely nonfunctioning student who shows no interest in anything, who wears long sleeves and pants in 110-degree Tucson temperatures, whose dad died when she was an infant, whose mother died just last February, who is now living with her sister?

Tell those teachers about the deaths?

About how she just moved from the Marshall Islands and knows almost zero English?

Nah, we have to think about FERPA, people.

These days checking mail is just a twenty-first-century computer click away rather than a trip to the teacher workroom, where pink slips of paper used to protrude from our boxes telling us what happened While You Were Out, screaming Call Back and Urgent from nervous parents needing comfort.

I go now only to check on suspension paperwork for Abel.

The walk toward the office is a mixture of the syrupy smell of pancakes wafting from the cafeteria and the bleachy scent of a janitor's freshly made mop bucket ready for the postapocalyptic morning of nine hundred children in a feeding frenzy.

A stack of Disneyland fliers, a pack of karate school handouts, and more Scholastic Book packets than I have students crowd my own personal six-by-nine rectangle, but there's nothing that says why Abel is out.

I check the basket where I laid Manny's paperwork last night, still resting comfortably, no rush to pick it up, his schoolwork not escaping anytime soon.

Behind me I hear, "Manny was part of that drug bust, right?"

I don't have to turn around to know it's Amanda Weiss, the most inspirational social studies teacher in the history of pubescent self-gratification and an example of why I love email so much.

Last year she wanted one of my students retained.

"I'm concerned he won't be successful," said Mrs. Weiss.

"Maybe he'll be grateful we did this for him," said Mr. Ward.

Yes, yes, Mr. Ward. That's the word I was looking for as well. Grateful like those native tribes on the West coast were so grateful for those nice, warm blankets the US calvary gave them.

"His mother died years ago, and his dad just died a month ago," I said.

"So you think he should get a free pass?" said Weiss, daughter of Nathan and Greta Weiss, granddaughter of Dr. and Mrs. Weiss, all still alive, all still attending Friday-night family dinners.

I wanted to let her know there was no such thing as a free pass, tell her that the tragedies bestowed on this boy will not be cured by another year of eighth grade, but she didn't want to hear what I had to say about retention. The fact that retention has shown to negatively affect student achievement is not something many teachers want to discuss.

"I'm not sure who was involved," I say to Weiss.

There's a fervor to her voice. She's antidrug, antichaos, anti-Manny. "He ditched my class his first day—I have a friend who works at the school where he came from, and she said he was a menace," she says. "I guess he ran away from the vice principal and threw food at the principal."

"Oh," I say, because I'd rather have a root canal than stand here talking to Weiss. I consider saying something congenial. Instead I say, "See you later," as I walk out of the mailroom and head back to my room.

When I was an undergraduate in the first semester of my education classes, Ed pulled me aside and whispered in my ear, "Autonomy." He leaned in closer, "Decorate the room, arrange the desks and cabinets and cubbies as you like, shut the door, and teach as you wish."

I scribbled in my notebook, "autonomy."

Drew little hearts around it.

He didn't mention I would use my autonomy to avoid teachers like Ward and Weiss, my classroom a haven from teachers whose philosophies conflict with my own.

After grading a few papers and sipping a bit more coffee, I swing open my door just in time for the first passing period bell to ring.

"It is Friday, right?" I say.

"Yeah, we made it," says Maggie. "But I think someone added a day to this week—it's like we're doing Friday twice."

I disagree. We did Wednesday twice, and Thursday never ended.

"Did you see the eclipse email?" I say. "Pacheco called it a 'unique opportunity' and then told us no one can take their students out unless we're teaching a designated science class."

"Well, it makes sense—if you can't control the kids, you might as well control the sun," says Maggie. "And really, it's just an eclipse—there will be another one."

Yesterday Destiny asked if something was bothering me.

I looked at her in the front row, pencil in hand, lined paper ready to be filled. I saw the blue was beginning to fade, but she had done her hair a little differently Thursday morning.

"Who did your hair?" I asked.

"Oh," she said, "I'm trying a little something new." She reached back and showed me the tiny ponytail she had on the back of her head, a few wisps of hair pulled through a hair tie meant for more hair than hers.

It was off-center.

"Aw, that's cute," I said. "I like it."

Destiny didn't know I was avoiding her question and not just her question but my answer. I had to teach despite the empty seats.

Gero's head came through the door, and I immediately sent him back into the hallway to ask him what happened. My fourteen-year-old informant has impeccable reconnaissance, FERPA not a concern for teenage tattletales.

The information he gives makes me go a little easier on him since he won't read for me. At all. Like not even a sentence.

"I don't know. I think Manny brought stuff to school, and he was selling it in the bathroom," he said.

"What about Abel?"

"I think he just likes to smoke it, but he don't sell it. That'd be stupid."

"What about you?" I looked at him in my detective stance, holding onto my interrogation stare.

"Aw, Ms. You know me," he says. "I wouldn't do that. You've seen my mom?" He said it like a question, but there is no question. "She'd smack me with her *chankla* if I did something like that."

He wasn't lying. I've met her.

As my second period enters, it's apparent by the empty seats that I'm still missing a few students. The smell of marijuana lingers in the air.

There is no official school communication as to why Abel was gone for two days, no request for homework, no explanation as to his involvement in the drug bust; my most reliable informant still fourteen-year-old Gero.

Abel is the last one through the door.

We knuckle bump as he passes. He saunters by with the same indiscernible face, sits at his desk, pulls out his book, and starts to read.

I want to be mad, relentlessly tough on him, so he can see the error of his ways, but when I look closer, I see he's halfway through his book.

Abel read at home.

As I head for my desk, I reach for my chest and wonder silently if anyone in this room would know how to call 911, and then I remember Destiny is in here. She'd save me.

"Abel," I say. "Come here."

He looks up at me. I open my hands like a book so he knows what I want.

Maybe I wouldn't even ask Abel over if it hadn't been for Sabrina. Maybe I would have protected myself, kept my bubble distance from the boy with the bucket full of failing grades and a pool full of potential, but it's too late. There have been too many Sabrinas before him and just this peek, the sight of the pages he's read, gives me hope worth more than payday Friday.

"What's up?" he says. He's smiling. He's cute when he smiles. It breaks up the seriousness of his face, but it's funny he's smiling. He just came back from some sort of suspension, and he's probably still failing classes. How can he be smiling?

I point to my stool for him to sit, making sure he knows we're chatting again, positive he knows I'm not letting up the pressure.

"How's the grades?" I say quietly; this is not a sales session, like Monday with Manny.

"I talked to Sommers," he says.

"And?"

"I'm going to do test corrections at lunch today," he says.

I ask him about his other classes, and he answers the same, taking care of things, getting work turned in on time.

"But you haven't been here since Tuesday," I say.

"I went in this morning to Sommers's."

Kids at my school do test corrections, just not kids like Abel.

"Okay, keep it up," I say, as if it happens all the time. "Let me see your book—what page are you on?"

Even at this moment I must still be hesitant. I have had dozens of students fake read to the end of their books, unable to answer any questions only because they were trying to impress me.

Just as I did last time, I choose a page a few pages before Abel's bookmark.

"Ready?" I say.

He smiles.

I read quietly, prompting him to answer quietly. I cannot afford for him to answer incorrectly within anyone's earshot. Manny isn't here to listen, but everything we've already built will be set back for days if he cannot answer.

When I finish he says, "Oh, that's in chapter sixteen."

Abel talks, giving details I never predicted, telling me much more than I ever wanted to know about Tyrell and his two girl-friends. "I don't like Jasmine," he says.

I can't help but ask why not, and he continues on with more detail than I have time hear and more explicit than I want to know.

I stop Abel a few sentences into his spiel. "That's good—you're good."

Now I know why he's smiling.

"Nice work," I say, and I pat him on the knee. "Perfect. I'll ask you another question after the weekend, okay?"

He nods his head and gets up to leave but then turns and asks me for a bookmark.

"I don't have any," I say. It's embarrassing, of course, the reading teacher has no paper placeholders.

"That's okay," he says. "I'll just rip a paper out of the recycle bin."

This reading journey is much different than the one with Hector, the first smiley boy holding onto *Tyrell*. By the time he was in my class, he had already made every mistake a teenager could possibly make. Maybe he wasn't as interested in adding more to his juvenile court file, but when I told him the same thing, he nodded his head.

"I got you," he said.

"Also, Hector," I added. "There's something else I want you to think about—all last year, all that time, you were proving how much control you needed. When you break that cycle and decide to control yourself, what happens?"

"What do you mean?" he said.

I explained what he had accomplished so far, finishing *Tyrell* and *Bronxwood* in record time, handing in all his assignments in record time as well.

"How does it feel," I said, "to be in charge?"

"Good, I guess."

"Really? Just good? Normally you don't mind being sent out of the room, told how to sit and where to sit? Normally that's fine with you?"

He just looked at me, not quite getting what I was saying, and then he said, "Yeah, I like being in charge."

I need to have this same conversation with Abel, point out how it feels to be the one making decisions, ask him to consider the happiness he felt reading on his own, the pride he felt going to Sommers.

I stop short of asking how it felt to follow Manny into the bathroom.

On the surface our conversation appears to go well; one cannot say for sure, however. The teenage brain is in the middle of a growth spurt, unpredictable at best, unreliable at worst.

There's a crew heading to happy hour after work, but I decline.

"I thought you were the one who wanted to get drunk," Maggie says.

"Not just one night. It's all the nights," I say, and I laugh even though it's tragic, weeks like these.

This day I head to my pop's house for my own Friday family dinner. We're much like the Weiss family, only none of my grandparents are still alive, my actual parents have been divorced over forty years, and my father raised my four brothers and me almost completely by himself.

He's such a good guy I almost feel bad about blaming him, in the remodeled version of my childhood home, for one of the longest weeks of my life. "It's all your fault; you made me into a teacher," I say.

"That bad, huh?" he says, but he doesn't mean it. He's just using this opportunity to tell me one of his favorite stories about having his own school district's superintendent's son in his class. "You just had to laugh about it—or it'd make you cry," he says. "The superintendent's son was supposed to go to Coyote Trails, but he was such a horse's ass, they sent him to my school on his own special bus." He shakes his head then starts to chuckle. "Superintendents," he says, "shoot, I bet that guy wasn't even supposed to be at your school."

All of our conversations are like this; the only difference is the superintendent's son is the only story in his repertoire where the student isn't the hero.

"You know—all that other stuff—the superintendent, the principal trying to stop the eclipse—you just gotta focus on the kids like that Abel kid you're talking about—keep focusing on him. That's all that matters."

"Tell me the one about the kid you got to read *Stone Fox* and all the other kids were cheering for him."

"You mean the kid who couldn't figure out the word, 'oatmeal,' that was written down was the same oatmeal you'd eat? That kid—well he came late to my room that year—he was in trouble pretty much every day ..."

It's definitely one of my favorite stories. My dad is full of them, and he tells them over and over again: the boy who learned how to read with the whole class cheering him on, the girl who got to the front of the lunch line every day for going to the neighbor's house to shower since her own home's water had been turned off, the time he helped the family burn their lice-infested couch, the time he combed a ratted knot out of a girl's hair.

"We're so grateful," said her parents. "She wouldn't let us near it."

A fifth-grade teacher in one of Arizona's poorest rural areas, my dad was part teacher, part therapist, part nurse, part philanthropist, and all disciplinarian.

As I drive to my own house, I remember I never answered Destiny.

It's a little too late, but I'd like to answer her now.

I'd tell her about my dad, of course, tell her one of the stories from his litany.

It would be so obvious I was raised on school.

School runs through my veins and courses through the marrow of my bones.

Everything about me says "school."

I believe in school.

"The problem is, Destiny," I'd say, "despite my belief in my profession, despite my unwavering dedication to your class-mates, despite my utter obsession with all you little pookies going to college, I have more students heading for dropout than graduation."

5

COMPLIANCE

Manny's suspension does nothing to improve his attendance. When he does show back to school, he's out of uniform.

"He wouldn't change shirts, eh?" I say to Mark in the in-house suspension room.

"Nope," he says, pointing over to the corner, where I see my hoodie-covered student.

It is evident Manny does not shower at the same rate as Abel, nor does anyone in his home feel the necessity to launder clothes as often as one might prefer their clothes to be laundered, his preference for this out-of-uniform shirt and sweatshirt quite a testament to just how unappealing his uniform clothes must be right now...wadded up on a floor somewhere in an overcrowded apartment...

It's an olfactory challenge to move close to him, but that doesn't stop me.

This boy and the one everyone has written about on the computer are two different boys. Under his name multiple teachers have lodged multiple complaints about Manny's behavior: he doesn't finish work if he starts work; he throws paper, pencils, erasers, books, and Takis; and he cusses and complains and whines about needing tissue for his nose, the restroom for his overactive bladder, the nurse for his tummy ache, and a Band-Aid for his tiny cut, the counselor because he's not happy with life, and the principal because he's not happy with the teacher.

The latest complaint said, "Manny walked out of class today and said he was going to see the principal. He stated frustration with me over my refusal to allow him to use the restroom because he never came back the day before when I did let him go. I confirmed later that he was with the principal the rest of the class period and the next until lunchtime, when I saw him by the basketball court."

The social studies teacher wrote this latest entry.

I respect Ms. Rodriguez for her dedication and determination, but more importantly as one of the only teachers I know who is more intense than I am. If I need a parent called in Spanish, I ask Bella Luisa. She can make a call home about throwing spit wads or lying or cheating or blatant disrespect sound like a Gatling gun firing in an elevator.

One year I caught a student texting, and when I confronted him and asked why he thought he could use his phone in my class, he said, "Ms. Rodriguez lets me."

I laughed. "Really? Because Ms. Rodriguez is so chill?"

The rest of the class laughed too.

She's as chill as a polar bear eating dinner with her cubs.

Ms. Rodriguez, "chill"—still funny, but what isn't funny is her intervention. She tried to control Manny's at-school truancy, and the principal rewarded Manny by spending time with him.

I doubt I'd be treated with the same hospitality if I were to walk out.

But teachers don't tell principals how to handle discipline, and despite the fact administrators deal with discipline daily, I don't think Ed talked about it either.

After the initial stage of triage in the ER, the doctor determines the next step in the intervention of death. In my principal's case, this would be a hug and a comfy chair.

I'm not so chill.

I tap Manny on the shoulder so he knows I'm there. He picks up his head, and I make a motion with my hand so he knows he can't wear the hoodie while we talk.

He pushes his hood back and says, "What's up?" like we're pals meeting on a street corner, two dudes at the park for a game of basketball. I ignore his attempt to minimize the situation.

"You in here for a while?" I say.

"I don't know."

I look up at Mark, who's listening, always observant, the overseer who also doesn't do chill. "He's in here today and maybe tomorrow. They haven't told me yet."

I look back at Manny. "Okay, well you'll have time."

"Time for what?" he says.

"Time to read this." I put the book down in front of him.

He picks it up, looks at the cover, and says, "It looks gay."

I laugh because he's right. Not that it looks gay, but that it is a terrible, terrible cover. "Your vocabulary sucks, but the book doesn't. I promise."

"What's it about?"

"Dude stuff," I say. "It's a dude's book. I give it to more students than any of my books. You'll like it. I swear."

"I don't read."

"Right. You don't, and I'm pretty sure you lost my copy of *The Bully*, didn't you?"

"I don't know," he says. "Maybe."

"Well, you can, and you will read this, or I will sit here next to you if that's what it takes. I'll get a sub and be your best friend aaaaaaaall day, right here." I hear Mark chuckle behind me. He knows me, I know him; we can do this all day long. "You know I'm not kidding, right?"

This time Manny laughs. "Yeah, I can tell."

"Good," I say. "I'll come back to check on you. And, Mark? You let me know if I need to come back earlier; otherwise, I'll be back after fifth."

"Cool," he says. "I doubt we'll have any problems, and I'll ask him questions—make sure he's reading." He smirks at Manny. "We're good, right?"

Manny nods, and I head back to a colleague's classroom.

Tuesday mornings are set aside for morning administrative meetings, our time to sit in desks and listen to the latest lecture series, part of our contract, a tiny footnote at the bottom of the page vowing our educational compliance.

"We have work to do, people," says el jefe.

Rumor has it, Benchmark tests tell us where we are in our teaching and where our students are in their learning, and they predict where we will be in five months if we don't shape up.

"You need to conference with each student in your homeroom class about bringing up their test scores and getting a few more correct. Remember, we are going for 80 percent."

He used to coach baseball. I want to ask him if that was his batting advice. "Did you say, 'swing better,' or did you actually instruct on how to hit a ball? I'm confused. How do we explain, 'get more right' to a twelve-year-old?"

Our local Tucson newspaper reporter suggested the teachers from the north side schools with higher scores could bring their teaching skills to the south side and garner the same results.

My dad's principal had a similar theory, thought she'd bring in some *master teachers* to handle the discipline problems in the school and to help the kids bubble better.

Within three months the self-proclaimed gurus sat in the

cafeteria, lamenting their inability to know what to do with the sundry of problems at the school, when my dad walked up and sat at the table.

"You ask," whispered one.

"No, you ask," whispered another.

"No. You ask," said the third.

Finally, my dad said, "How can I help you, ladies?"

After a number of elbows to the ribs, one of them said, "How do you do it? How do you handle these kids? They are so wild. We have no idea what to do. We tried prizes and parties and celebrations, and nothing works. Just yesterday I had a girl take a cupcake off my desk without asking and pop it in her mouth."

My dad nodded his head. "Yeah, that happens."

"All the kids steal cupcakes?"

He laughed. "No, all the kids are not stealing cupcakes, but it happens."

"Well, what do you do? Tell us what to do. We need to know."

"I have a system that works," he said.

"What is it?"

"Well, it's kind of controversial, but I think you'll find it to be pretty effective."

He leaned in, whispering low, dragging it out, making it seem like NASA had the idea hidden under lock and key.

They leaned in, too, wanted to know what the real master teacher was going to say.

"First, you take the worst boy in the group," he said. "I mean the toughest one of those suckers—and you grab ahold of him in one hand and you grab your best stapler in the other—you better check it first because the new ones break too easily, so use an old heavy metal one and make sure it has staples—then with one in one hand and one in the other, you have one shot to staple that boy's nuts to his leg."

Three slack-jawed masters watched as my dad picked up his lunch tray and walked out the door.

My principal knows the teachers on Tucson's north side aren't getting their scores because of the teachers. Their letter grade comes from the test-passer parents who birthed test-passing babies.

Where I work the problem lies in the cognitive disconnect between test parties; the cultural majority creates the test for the cultural minority.

Imagine all those little test makers taking a test written by members of the Navajo Nation. What subtleties would be misunderstood? Complexities of language and thought so inherently linked to culture that the professional test makers may, I dare say, flunk the test?

Outrageous!

Unheard of!

Not in my state!

But it's possible, isn't it?

Teachers, real teachers, don't test to assign letter grades. We test to assess the learning that has occurred in order to ascertain the learning that is still needed.

Districts test in order to predict the results of state tests.

States test in order to label school districts and schools: A, B, C, and Failing.

How do you go from Failing to A?

Get more right!

Hit more balls!

I don't know why I'm so worried. I'm doing my job teaching kids how to read three-hundred-page books completely independently, remember every detail, comprehend the cause and effect of characters' actions, understand the metaphors and the similes, know the development of the plot, and engage in text like they are jumping into a pool…Oh, but wait. They aren't being tested on all of that. That's the problem. Oh yeah, now I remember why I'm so worried.

I'm just going to tell them to swing harder, better, faster. Like the nonreaders I have who start with *Drive By*, the ones I need to teach to read, then to love books. *Those*—I'm going to tell *those* kids—to hit more balls.

Now I sit with Manny, but he's not a can't-reader, just a nonreader.

Besides, for his test scores from fourth grade, a child who understands words on the page looks much different than the one who cannot. One registers confusion, the other understanding. The difference with Manny is, his face registers fear and defiance, but I don't care.

Times like these it's important to note I have two diplomas stating Ed and I spent a lot of time together.

One of my engineer friends says my classes were all easy. "Didn't you all just do group projects and sit around singing 'Kumbaya'?"

I told him no, but I was only being defensive. We were education majors—if we weren't singing 'Kumbaya,' we were constructing group projects.

The summer of '96 was no different. Our final for LRC410 was to present *Savage Inequalities* by Jonathan Kozol.

Simple.

We'd done our share of projects: culled out important info, presented what we learned in some charismatic fashion, waited for the applause, bowed, sat down, and waited for the next group to present.

We had this.

The book highlights the travesty of an educational system designed to segregate and isolate. Our clever group made two game boards. One represented St. Louis and the other, East St. Louis. We created two versions of The Road to Graduation!

With pencil we drew the board for East St. Louis; with torn scraps of paper, we made drawing cards with data from the book.

1. The school's sewage system is backed up. All students must evacuate the campus. Move back two spaces.
2. Your fifth-grade class has run out of school supplies. Use a crayon for your writing assignment.
3. Your school has just received your state test scores, and you earned a D. Drop out or move back to square one.

With markers and glitter, we created a second board to represent St. Louis, with index cards we made drawing cards with data from the book.

1. Your school has just updated their technology. Move up three spaces.
2. Your principal just won Principal of the Year and was written up in the paper.
3. You just received a new textbook, and your friends are getting together to do a textbook-drive for the East St. Louis school you keep hearing so much about.

We moved the St. Louis game by the window to absorb the sun streaming through the classroom windows and we turned the lights down low on East St. Louis.

We used Monopoly game pieces for St. Louis, and we tore more pieces of scrap paper for East St. Louis. Then we realized we only had one die.

"Give it to the St. Louis game board. I'll tell East St. Louis what they rolled," someone said.

"Good idea!" someone else said.

With less thought than we'd put into our coffee orders, four members of the University of Arizona's Department of Education started their presentation.

I stood next to the game board as my group buddy crossed his arms and told the players what they rolled.

"Two," he said.

"What? What are you doing?" someone said.

"You rolled a two, now move or lose your turn," he said.

With their heads down, they moved, they read their ripped-paper cards, they moved again.

"My textbook doesn't have a cover. Move back two spaces."

"My school ran out of breakfast. I didn't get to eat. Move back one space."

The roll master never let them move more than three spaces.

From where we were, we could hear the players from St. Louis with their sunshine and glitter.

There was clapping. "My school just got new school supplies. Yes!"

They teased each other. "My school just got a new computer lab! Awesome! Move up three spaces!"

They saw their future. "Better watch out! If I roll a six, I graduate!"

We were presenters, not research scientists. We predicted none of this. We wanted As, nothing more.

We looked at our watches. We had ten minutes left for our presentation.

"What should we do?" someone said.

Our grade could be affected. We hadn't planned for time.

"Let's have them switch sides and play for ten more minutes," someone said.

Again, another great idea made with no more thought than

how much creamer to pour into that coffee, how much sugar to sprinkle and stir.

The St. Louis graduates laughed their way over to our East St. Louis board.

"What's this game?" someone said.

"Oh! It's just like the other one," someone else said. "Where's the die?"

"I'm telling you what you rolled," said the Roll Master, an unforeseen eminence emerging. "There are no dice here," he said, puffy chested, condescension dripping from his tongue. "You rolled a three."

"A three?"

"Yes, a three. You have a problem with that?" he said.

If they had a problem, they never said so.

The difference between the first set of gamers and the second was insignificant. Their complacency arrived quickly and stayed for the duration, but across the room we heard a strange transition from east to west.

"What? We can roll?" someone said.

"Five?" someone said. "I can move five?"

"Six? I can move six spaces? Are you kidding?"

They questioned every card they read.

"We got new textbooks?"

"It says we get new computers and I get to move three spaces. That doesn't seem right. What's the catch?"

There was no catch. We didn't even know what we were doing. Like every presentation I'd ever had as a college student, we planned it last minute, and half the group didn't even read the book.

But I did.

I knew how bad the situation was in East St. Louis.

But I didn't.

Toward the end of the game with the glittery St. Louis game board, I looked over just in time to see a player set her game piece on the übersparkly CONGRATULATIONS! space.

"Oh, great. I graduated," she said, her head resting in her free hand. "Now what?" she added.

My sentiments exactly, Mr. Kozol.

Now what?

I was raised fifty feet from a trailer park with more boards than glass. There were six of us on a teacher's salary, four of whom could make an entire pork shoulder, potatoes, and corn on the side look like an appetizer.

I thought I knew something about being poor, but then, one poorly planned, ill-prepared presentation later, I realized I know nothing about poverty.

Back in Mark's room, I sidle up next to Manny, and looking over his shoulder, I see he's made quite the dent in *The Absolutely True Diary of a Part-Time Indian.*

"How is it?" I say.

"Good, I guess," he says.

"Good? Come on, seriously? It's better than good—"

"I guess," he says.

From the tiny smirk circling the right side of his face to the squint of his eyes, everything about him says he's lying. Manny may be a lot of things, but a poker player is not one.

"He'll be here another day," says Mark.

"Awesome," I say. "That'll give you time to finish and then we'll see if you still say it's just 'good.'"

I put my hand on Manny's shoulder as I stand to leave, my teacher reflex to bridge the gap between our ages, our stations in life. I don't need to spend even a minute in Manny's home to know the two seconds my hand spends on his shoulder is the only positive touch he will feel all day.

But I'm not going soft; it's a rouse—it's always a rouse. If I get him to read this book, he won't ever be able to undo what he read. No way to get out of Manny's system the words of a boy who overcomes obstacles much larger than the ones Manny sees.

I'm not chill. Chill doesn't work. I have one shot with Manny, and I'm going to shoot.

6

ONE UP

*"A book is less important for what it says
than what it makes you think."*

—LOUIS L'AMOUR

Sixty-five days into school and it's time to crank up the crazy;
teachers, like farmers, are susceptible to the elements of wind,
rain, and snow and, unlike farmers, holidays.

"I'd like to take this moment to not thank the Celts for
the invention of Halloween," I say to my next-door neighbor,
Cruella De Vil. "You do look great, by the way."

"Why, thank you—and you're dressed as what? What do
you call that?"

"I told you, I'm dressed as a teacher, a really, really
casual teacher."

"But you wear jeans, flip-flops, and the school polo every day."

"Yeah, well, I didn't want to scare the kids by wearing shoes.
They'd think we had a sub and probably ditch my class."

The candy hasn't even hit the bag yet, and our kids are little
freaks running in the hallway, hitting each other on the head,
screaming and yelling for no climactic reason.

"Wait till Monday," says Cruella.

She's right; in two days' time, we'll be scraping chocolate off
our floors and sweeping away empty wrappers in our attempts

to keep calm and order during our behemoth three-week testing march.

In the past we used pencil and paper, but the district decided to make the technological switch to computers last year, creating a computer-juggling impossibility for most schools and a serious coordinating conundrum for our school.

"I think I slept three hours last night," el jefe told us. "I don't know how we're going to do this, people, but we're going to do this, people."

"Hit more balls," I whispered to Maggie.

"Swing like you mean it," she whispered back.

We were in el jefe's pretesting emergency meeting before school this morning.

He calls a last-minute get-together every testing session in order to reiterate the same protocol procedures he's already reiterated: the snack updates, the bathroom-break schedules, the cell-phone containment modus operandi, emergency contact numbers in case there has been a breach of testing etiquette.

"The library won't be open again until after Thanksgiving," I said to Maggie.

"Books are overrated," she said.

My friends are jerks.

She's joking, but the juggling nightmare isn't just about the computers. The library is where they take all the testing slackers, who spend five hours or more of their day staring at the computer screen trying to decide between A, B, C, or D.

Getting teens and preteens to finish first and second and the third books in their lives is hard enough with the library open.

Before I head to class, I stop by Mark's to check on Manny.

His back is to me when I walk into the room, but I can see he has on a blue polo. His shorts have never been in question;

he wears the same khaki shorts every single day. I know this because there are stains that never change.

I point to Manny as I look at Mark, my brows raised in a question—shock really. Manny is in uniform?

"Yep," he says. "He let us get him a shirt today, so I guess he'll be back in class tomorrow—if he wears the shirt again."

His hair looks washed too, and there's the definite scent of soap wafting from his skin, making it remarkably easy to scooch closer. I pull up a chair and squeeze into the booth where he's reading.

"Dude," I say. "What the heck?" I point to the right side where only a few pages lie unread.

"I'll finish today," he says.

"Obviously. When did you read all of that?"

"I don't know—last night, I guess."

Last night.

I guess.

I cannot comprehend.

And even if I wanted to, I don't have time.

Teachers don't really get a chance to be happy, at least where I work. I cannot spend time rejoicing over the pages Manny says he's read because I'm terrified he's lying, relying on my lazy nature to let this boy slide, let him fake read.

"Let's talk about Ted," I say.

"The dude with the dress? Sure, what do you want to know?"

What do *I* want to know?

The confidence radiating from Manny's face could light a thousand thousand-watt bulbs lighting a dark street, a darker forest, the darkest cavern.

"I'll come back after lunch so we have a chance to talk." I put my hand on his shoulder to stand, but I don't need the help. "Nice work," I say. "I'm impressed."

Back at my door as I take my key out, Destiny walks up with a small plate with a tin-foil cover.

More than once my dad told me, "If a student offers you food, you have to accept."

More than once I've accepted food of questionable origin.

"I made it myself," she says, smiling as if she'd ground the flour, milked the cow, and gathered the eggs.

My worry about the cleanliness of her kitchen, the bacteria festival on her fingertips, and the salmonella swimming in the eggs is no longer relevant. She killed my excuses with her face, that bright, beautiful face.

Dammit. I really wanted to fit into these jeans in May.

I pull back the foil exposing what appears to be a Rorschach-inspired pumpkin, orange frosting stuck to the foil, white frosting ready to head toward my belly. Destiny says she has a few more pieces to deliver, and I sweep her away with my hand, no need to speak, my mouth is full of cake, and I need to plot my next sentence to Maggie.

I'm torn between a *lamenting waistline* haiku or a *kids make me fat* limerick when Mark walks up.

"Did you hear?" he says.

Did I hear about the teacher who finally got caught leaving his students unattended?

Or did I hear about the bag of marijuana hidden underneath the tampon-and-bloody-pad trash in the girls' eighth-grade hallway?

Maggie scoots into the circle, Rodriguez walks by, sees the huddle, walks back, another teacher sidles in, and it's official: an impromptu meeting of the One-Up Club has commenced.

"Was it the girl fight?" someone says.

"The boy fight?" says someone else.

"The girl who propositioned all the boys to meet her in the bathroom?"

"Cervantes is out again, and we all have to cover for her?"

So many possibilities, so little time, the ticktock of passing period increases our fervor.

"Was it the bus driver who slammed on his breaks, sending a student flying forward into another seat?"

"Damon?"

"Yeah."

"Not sure I wouldn't have done the same."

What about the six-inch knife that was documented as two inches long for too-many-suspensions sake?

Or that MUSD screwed up with so many people's paychecks they have to offer emergency checks to five hundred people?

Finally, someone says, "We give up."

"Jesus," he says.

Oh, well, that narrows it down.

Was it the crotch-grabbing incident, or the whole-hand-in-his-pants incident?

The simulated-masturbation incident, or the condom-on-the-banana incident?

So many offenses, so little time to guess.

"Was it when he yelled, '*La encontré aguada*,' across the room in Rodriguez's room?"

"What does that mean?" says Mark.

"I found her wet."

"Seriously?"

"Seriously."

"Well," says Mark, "I haven't even heard of a few of those, but yesterday he told Pacheco he needed to grow a pair."

That makes us laugh.

"What'd Pacheco do about it?"

"Sent him home for two days."

The bell rings, ending passing period.

It's probably better this way. The curse words set to spew from my mouth are not meant for classrooms or hallways or any other space within the school boundaries.

We disperse ourselves silently, none of us truly understanding how blatant sexual offenses are lower on the hierarchical behavior tree than a student stating the truth.

Mark is about to walk away when he turns back and says, "Hey, I meant to tell you." He comes closer, avoiding the last-second children sprinting into rooms. "Turns out it also looks like Jesus is the one who brought the pot."

"Oh, really?" I say. "And he didn't get caught?"

"Nope. No one told on him—guess what else?"

I just look at my friend, no idea what's next with the winner of today's one-up competition.

"Remember when that guy kidnapped those two girls on the south side? Kept them locked up in his hotel room—drugged them—made them do unspeakable things?"

He leans back and looks at me.

I'm already speechless.

"That's Manny's dad," he says.

The spiral of fifth-grade Manny needs no more explanation.

A town like Tucson doesn't often have reported crimes this heinous. The arresting officers referred to him as an *animal*; at sentencing the judge called his actions *barbaric*.

"Geezus," I say. "Don't talk to me anymore, okay?"

I walk into my room and immediately begin to focus on my computer, my emails, my attendance, listening and not listening to the conversations around me, vigilantly eavesdropping for F-bombs, S-bombs and sexual-orientation name-calling while simultaneously hoping I don't hear any.

Within a few minutes, the entire class settles down and begins reading. Abel, the budding reader, is next to Gero, the book flipper.

I'm taking attendance on the computer when I hear Abel say, "Dude, why don't you read?"

Gero's response to Abel's heckling is inaudible if there is one.

They are both sitting directly in front of my desk. I've never read *Tyrell*, but my students say the ending is intense. Without looking I can sense Abel's shaking head, hear the disappointment in his old beliefs, his disappointment in boys in general, his frustration with Gero.

"You're an idiot for not reading this," says Abel.

I laugh out loud, and Abel hears me. "Ms.?" he says. "Sorry, I didn't mean for you to hear that."

"Are you kidding?" I say. "That's the best thing I've heard all week."

I don't tell him his little side comment calling out his friend may be the only thing keeping me from jumping out my first-story window, running, arms flailing, screaming, "It's too much! This job is too much!" from every pore of my body…

The front page of this morning's paper actually started my day in this painful educational arch. It seems we have a new chairwoman for the Senate Education Committee who will decide the fate of legislative education proposals.

According to the article, Stacey Alton possessed three qualities essential to her appointment: ingenuity, determination, and emotional strength. Spending even a moment as a classroom teacher was not a requirement.

Thank goodness though, because a day like today would have damaged her beyond repair, even the idea of being the chairwoman for education too much to endure after one day in an actual classroom.

I look back at Abel. "You seriously changed your perspective on girls? That's amazing."

I wish I could tell Ms. Alton what Abel just said and what it says about him as a person and as a reader, but I guess it wouldn't matter.

I'm just mad. I'm a teacher who wants to talk to a student about his book, and I don't have time.

I look back at Abel.

I look up at the clock.

El jefe has instructed us all to cover the testing protocols, so there's no time for teaching, for talking about a book that changed a boy's dating future.

Someone asks what we're doing today.

I tell them we're covering testing protocols.

Someone asks why we test; someone else asks what protocols are.

Three hands go up to use the restroom.

One student walks up and asks to go to the nurse.

One asks for a Band-Aid.

Another yells from the back of the room, "Have we eaten lunch yet?"

I'd pay fifty dollars to see Madam Chairwoman go over the testing procedures with my students. I'd sit in the back, sipping my coffee, eating crumb cake, and videotaping the entire lesson. I'd love to see her pick up broken pieces of crayon off the floor as she explains why we test and how preparing for these tests and taking these tests are worth every single minute of time, every single dollar spent.

I'd make sure she knew about Manny's past, about Jesus's present, and about Abel's future.

Maybe Madam Chairwoman and I could go have drinks afterward and she could explain to me just how important testing is, what it actually measures and what we do with those measurements.

Then, when she was good and drunk, maybe five rum and Cokes later, I'd ask her just how much money changes hands between the Department of Education and Pearson Education. I'd like to know if she knows the largest testing company of American children is a British company.

I'm so excited I think of applying online for a job in the test-making business. Of course, it would be more than I'm making now, but I'm probably not qualified.

Teaching wouldn't be a necessary background requirement.

Teacher daydreams are a distraction.

I don't have time for distractions. I must cover the protocols as soon as possible.

We only have a day before the test, and anyone in education knows that we need to practice testing so we can test.

By the end of the day I feel as though I'm drowning in a pool of test booklets, but I make it back to Manny anyway.

As I walk into Mark's room, he's walking out. "I need to check on a kid," he says. Then he points at Manny and smiles.

As I get closer to Manny, I see his book is next to him, a sheet full of unfinished fractions on the desk in front of him, scribble marks on the top right hand corner, no name, nothing showing he's accomplished a single thing all day.

"Hey," I say.

"Hey," he says back.

This job can be so overwhelming. No time to process what happens because the next thing is always happening. Kids read the first book of their lives, and I have to move on to the next kid, the one with the head down, the one passing out in front of me while I write the nurse's pass, the one with his hands in his pants.

But in Mark's room, it's just Manny and me.

No distractions.

"Did you finish?" I say.

"Yeah," he says.

"And?"

"It was cool."

It was cool.

The conversation is filled with short answers, but with depth too. Most students stick to simple plot pieces or favorite scenes. Manny's sense of story was far more intense than the average.

In the moment, like the rest of the day, it is too much to process.

Mark walks back into the room just as Manny and I finish talking.

"The District?" I say. "Half hour?"

"Of course," he says.

I'm grateful.

I need a drink.

Thirty minutes later Mark and I meet in the parking lot of Tucson's only school-themed bar, complete with bartending principals sporting polyester leisure suits and rule-wielding waiters ready to smack the hands of unruly customers.

"It doesn't smell like school," Mark says as we walk into the graffiti-flavored ambiance, original Tucson high school photos lining the walls.

"That's because teachers only drink vodka at school—it doesn't have an odor, remember?—oh, look, it's your high school girlfriend," I say as I point to one of the many senior photos splashed around the room, bring-your-own photo part of The District's appeal.

"Um, I think that was your girlfriend," he says.

"The one with the mullet?" I laugh. "It's possible."

We decide on the bar since all the tables are full of other miserable commiserating public school employees. Not all of course; some customers are just normal people with normal jobs.

A few people are in costume, silly string cobwebs and giant dangling spiders hang from the ceiling; a flying witch hovers overhead.

"I totally forgot it was still Halloween," I say.

"How was your day?" Mark says as our glasses clink in Friday celebration, not hearing 'Ms.' three thousand times a day for two days reason enough to celebrate.

"Fine," I say, but I want to tell him about the fact Manny finished a book in twenty-four hours, about how he said it was cool, about how he already took his next book home. But I can't.

I don't know why.

Maybe I like to keep some things for myself; maybe I'm selfish.

Manny asked me why a character's dad beats him for losing a basketball game, and we talk about angry, drunken fathers.

I moved closer to him to try to see what he saw, feel what he felt.

I asked him if he remembered the rematch basketball game where Arnold played his old school. "Remember how he felt afterward?" I said.

"He threw up," he said.

I explained Man Versus Self, told him that Arnold had to forgive himself for what he did.

"But he just won a basketball game."

"Did he? Was that all? Or was it the culmination of a school year of fighting for himself?"

Manny acted like he didn't know what I meant, but he's a liar. Nobody reads a book in twenty-four hours, has adult conversations about the book, and then doesn't understand the implications of what was written.

"If you're going to play dumb," I said, "make sure you actually are dumb."

He laughed. "All right."

I looked at him. I couldn't help myself. I had to teach him more.

"Forgiving ourselves for deserving more is the hardest struggle we'll ever have," I said.

We talked about the literary importance of what I was saying, about Arnold's struggle, about Manny's struggles being in uniform, staying in class, respecting the adults around him.

I asked him why he thinks I want kids to read *True Diary*.

"I don't know," he said.

"Yeah, you do," I said. "Think about it."

"All right, I'll think about it."

Then I asked him if he wanted another book and he said, "Sure."

This couldn't be happening.

But it was happening.

I got it together, acted like everything was cool, as it should be, everyone who's in in-house reads, conversations like this happen every day all over America, no biggie. You're just like everyone else, Manny. You're good. We're good. Everyone reads a book in a day.

I said, "Okay, I'll bring you *Tyrell*."

I thought we were done. I picked up my copy of *True Diary*

and turned to leave, told him I'd see him later. "Maybe you can come in uniform Monday and be in class like everyone else."

He smiled and laughed a little when I said that.

"Ms.?" he said.

I stopped. Gave him all my attention, yet I thought it was nothing, just asking me if he could use the restroom or go to the nurse or any number of other things a child like Manny will do to get out of whatever he's doing, a constant movement to just not be here, wherever here is.

"Yeah?" I said. "What do you need?"

Then he said the unexpected, a kid like Manny with such a long drought of any school success, the terror that must have been his life since birth and the tragic events of his fifth-grade year, but I'm not telling Mark.

I'm keeping Manny's words for myself.

"Nothing," he said. "I just want to say thank you."

7

CHILL

Testing

/test/

1. *verb*

    1. take measures to check the quality, performance, or reliability of something especially before putting it into widespread use or practice.

I think about the cornfield hater on my way to work this morning, wondering if he knows the statistics of a child's brain on testing. A quick glance around my test-taking room, it's clear the tedious task of testing must deactivate the brain's firing mechanisms by 30 percent. I wouldn't know, of course. I'm just here testing these people.

There's a meme in my head: a classroom picture of my kids, the caption, "No one more in touch with these people," at the top. Next to my kids is another picture, the Queen of England, her teacup tipped slightly, her pinky raised modestly to the right, the caption, "… than these people."

Across the bottom, of course, "Pearson Education, the testing company that cares!"

If I plan this right, I'm thinking Pearson will get offended and have to rebrand the idea of testing, make it something gentler and more sensitive, the way "rape" became "assault," "killing" became "manslaughter," "death" became "passed away."

With a projector connected to my school computer, I

generate an image of a seventh-grade benchmark test, just a sample to show my students how to work through test questions, decoding in its base form.

I scroll down to the first question.

1. In the passage titled, "Who Killed Public Education," choose the answer that best explains what brought the demise of the public school system.

   A. Charter schools
   B. Pearson
   C. Group projects
   D. Your mom
   E. All the above

Of course, this isn't a real question. No true testing company would participate in such a smear campaign, their sensitivities far too delicate for propaganda of this magnitude.

When I finally have a break in my test-giving day, I'm summoned to Pacheco's office, but like a schoolgirl with a referral for fighting, I have to wait my turn.

Unlike a schoolgirl with fresh scrapes and bruises, remnants of some other girl's hair still between my fingers, I have no idea why I'm here.

I can hear Rodriguez through the windows, the doors, and the walls—Jesus's name is proceeded by curse words more than twice.

When she finally walks out, we don't exchange pleasantries, the possibility of us chillin' over drinks not in our near future.

As I walk into the room, Pacheco's hands are shuffling papers, the aftereffect of Hurricane Rodriguez. Despite Jesus's crime, Pacheco obviously dropped the offense down to a misdemeanor. If there were a betting pool on Jesus's punishment,

I'd say he received two days with Mark but only during Rodriguez's class.

A betting pool? Now that's an idea...

When Pacheco sees me, he leans back and folds his hands across his very tidy desk.

Like every principal I've ever known, his furniture is modest, his wall decorations educationally themed with awards and certificates, sans anything personal. If I were to guess the name of his cologne, it would probably be Ode de Sterile. There is no actual indication we are still in a school except that I appear to be in trouble.

Pacheco tells me Jason Henderson's mother didn't take too kindly to me taking a picture of her little pookie as he lay sleeping in my room, after lying, after not working, after not trying, after being on his phone, after lying and not trying and lying and not trying day after day after day.

She called el jefe and told him how awful I am.

"She says you showed the picture to the class," Pacheco says.

I remember this day. I was agitated, irritated with Jason's resignation to underachievement.

Maybe I'm always agitated.

"I showed the picture to him," I say.

"She says you humiliated him in front of the class."

I refrain from explaining that Jason falling asleep in class was what probably actually embarrassed Jason.

"Do you want me to call her?" I ask.

"No, thank you," he says. "Please refrain from this technique in the future. No need to call Mrs. Henderson. I'll make the call."

I leave moments after I arrive, no need to stick around thinking over every bad choice I've made as of late either.

Ed requires at least one behavior modification class before

graduation. I'm curious whether admin has their own, the difference between positive and negative reinforcement being *muy necessito* when divvying out wrist slaps and back pats.

"That's negative reinforcement," I say when Mark told me Pacheco was going to give Manny a five-hour schedule to reduce his time on campus.

"He was misbehaving most of the day, so now he's only here slightly more than half a day," he says.

"Last week Jesus was wearing jeans, and I told him to go to Pacheco," I tell Mark.

"Let me guess," he says. "Pacheco had already written him a free pass to wear them all day?"

"Positive reinforcement," I say.

El Grupo de la Pobrecitos is the name I give for teachers and admin who don't quite understand the art of discipline.

The poor little babies get ten minutes extra for lunch when they finally arrive to class on time, they get to wear beanies because they say they have a bad haircut, sunglasses because they say their eyes have a sensitivity problem, one detention for an infraction that would give another student three detentions.

And *el patronito de los pobrecitos*?

The one with the saddest story, the least to lose?

He gets a partial schedule.

"Manny's schedule, that's for real?" I say.

It is passing period, and Mark is standing with me and Maggie, coffees in our hands, eyes on the hallway traffic.

"Did you go to the meeting?" I say.

"Nope. I guess you didn't either."

"I wasn't invited," I say, and I doubt any of Manny's six other teachers were invited.

"That negative reinforcement really works," he says.

Don't get me wrong; there should be a group designated

to help the pobrecitos, but that is the job of the nurse and the community rep, not the warden and his guards, and if a parent wants to pass on the pobrecito gene, that's really none of our business, but we don't have to provide the diapers, wipes, and baby-rash ointment.

Three years ago I spent over an hour in the principal's office with two parents who insisted on meeting. Their daughter said I yelled at her in class and humiliated her.

I do actually do that. I've been known for outbursts of outrage at the slightest infractions. Just today I yelled at someone because he said the hallway smelled like fish.

I assumed he was making a sexual innuendo.

I was definitely making a teenage-boy generalization.

With Lisa I had to sit in a room with her parents and retell what happened. After just a few minutes, it was clear they'd rather I was a bad teacher than their daughter a bad liar.

We sat for an hour while I explained that I called Lisa over to my desk because I was concerned about her grades in three of her other classes. She became defensive and started yelling at me.

I told them I assumed something was bothering her, and I assured them it was not me.

I could see her parents struggling emotionally.

Her dad said, "When this all came up, her brother said you would never do what Lisa said."

Her mom said, "But Lisa isn't a liar."

For many it is much easier to give in to an angry thirteen-year-old than piss off the future sixteen-year-old. "Remember, Mom? Remember when you didn't believe me?"

Just ask Stephen King.

Weeks later when I vented to my hairdresser, she said her

son used to tell her his teachers weren't fair, and she'd tell him, "Suck it up, little dude. Just suck it up."

I have a professor friend who just posted on Facebook that parents should never come and talk to professors about their children.

But these examples aren't important. They're just parents and therefore cannot be privy to my exclusive club.

El Grupo is strictly a closed group for school personnel who acquiesce to the whims of teenagers.

Those with bars held high need not apply.

Later when I see Rodriguez again, it's during professional development. As Pacheco discusses the progress of Benchmark testing, I text Bella Louisa. "What happened to Jesus?"

She looks down and types back. "He's dead to me."

I have no words to console her. I send my friend a sad-face emoji and then a mad one while Pacheco tells us how we're running low on snacks, how we have had trouble with the Wi-Fi, trouble with lunch schedule, trouble testing all the children in a timely manner.

I refrain from telling him my ideas about Pearson; my anti-testing thoughts seem so sacrilegious here at school.

In my room the next day, I seek as much solace from Jason, Jesus, and testing as I can, a stolen assignment from a collection that began the day I decided to become a teacher. This particular one is my way of introducing the last few figurative vocabulary words from my curriculum.

My example will not earn me a poet laureate position even in Why, Arizona, population 350, but it's not for public viewing. It's just an example of letting my own vulnerability show. It is a ploy, after all. Sabrina taught me that much.

*Where I am from, there was one on-duty soldier, one
MIA*
> *Four combs and one brush*
> *Dirt clod fights and backyard climbing*
*Where I am from, there was a textbook destiny and
no-turning-back philosophy*
> *Rocky punches in the yard and spiral binders in
> the house*
> *After-school sports and summer road trips*
*Where I am from, sportsmanship rules, and quitting
isn't an option*
> *Saturdays were rakes and mowers*
> *Sundays were footballs and shooting ranges*
*Where I am from, doing always came first, and
talking came second*

Just the word *poetry* makes my students cringe with
thoughts of rhyming words and frilly flowers, but there are no
hops on pop or red roses in these poems. After a day or so, I get
some real thoughts I can use in my triage assessments.

Maria writes:

*Where I am from, there's red wine in a bottle and
Budweiser in a can*
> *Two bottles of nail polish and one blue diaper*
> *Three small fur coats and one big one*

Destiny writes:

*Where I am from, there are beans on the stove and
tortillas in the oven*
> *Shrines inside and shrines outside*
> *Love is sometimes a four-letter word*

I point to the "Love" line. "Clever," I say as I walk around the room, reading over shoulders. "Can I read that stanza out loud?"

She nods her head, and I say, "Here's another example," just loud enough to get everyone's attention. When I finish, I look at the next three lines and realize I have to read those too. "Where I'm from holidays aren't restricted by dates / Jelly beans at Christmas / Mistletoe on St. Patrick's Day."

Destiny looks up and smiles. "We're weird."

"And awesome," I say.

I continue walking, looking for more words to share.

Occasionally someone writes an entire poem that needs to be read, but everyone has a line or two that can be shared, a collective addition to the bar the class is raising together.

Then I get to Abel's.

> *Where I am from, there are more people than beds*
> *More mouths than food*
> *More rain than sun*

There's no teacher tool to help unlearn too much about a student, no rewind button, no rose-colored glasses to unsee what's already been seen.

"Hey," I say over his shoulder.

"Hey," he says. He looks up at me and back down to his paper.

I tap *mouths*. "Nice," I say, and keep walking, touching Abel's shoulder as I walk away.

I make my rounds through my cornfield rows, reading lines here and there, students from *quinceañeras* and Tejano music, cars on jacks, fathers gone, fathers home, lives gone awry, and a number of rewrites, just teaching students how to follow the pattern of the three-line stanza.

On my next trip around the room, I look again at Abel's paper. "Where I'm from dreams are stars and dirt is reality."

"Dude," I say. "You have like ten amazing lines. What the heck? Are you going to read the whole thing?"

"If you want," he says.

"Oh yeah, I want. In fact, I need you to come back and read to my other classes."

It's possible he knows I will not take no for an answer.

If I'm lucky, someone will want to change their poem, citing Abel's poem as their motivation for the change. When that happens, I can use that as an example too.

My father used to say all he needed was one great student and he could make an entire class.

"I'll email your teachers so you can come to all four of my other classes," I tell him. "That poem rocks."

I look at the clock and address the class. "Okay, everybody— the bell is about to ring. We're going to edit these tomorrow, practice reading them, and then Thursday and Friday we'll read them out loud."

"Do we have to read them out loud?" someone says.

My tree-hugging, peaceful, loving hippie side comes out during poetry week. Free-form slam poetry is one way I push them to examine their lives without judgment, but read them out loud?

The kids hate public speaking like no other.

"You can read or you can hire someone to read, and they don't have to read every line—just the parts you want is enough … except Abel. He has to read the whole thing."

There's more whining, of course. A number of people still saying, "Aw, Ms.? Do we have to?"

"It could be worse," I say. "We could be testing."

I expect someone to say, "Yeah, you're right," and somebody to say, "Good point, Ms., we'll stop complaining," but no one says a thing. My funniest line of the day falls flat on students who'd rather read random passages about remote lighthouses on the East Coast than talk about themselves and hear about their classmates.

I think of telling this story, but the enormity would be wasted on the three new teachers we bring to happy hour, and to be honest, it's much more fun to tell them how miserable they're about to be for the next four days.

"It's a teacher's curse," someone says.

"You're going to be sick the entire time, just wait," I tell them.

We're at happy hour, it's Wednesday, tomorrow is Thanksgiving, and that's what new teachers do.

Lie in bed for four days.

"Are you serious?" one of them says.

The rest of us agree. It happened to all of us.

I buy all three a drink, of course. It's the least I can do.

We got out of school early because we don't have to be developed professionally before we eat turkey and ham, rolls, and pie. Developing a resistance to alcohol is much more important.

We love The District for four reasons: First and second and third, we are comforted by the graffiti-covered walls and the loud music and louder patrons because it feels like work yet it's not work.

Fourth, there is no way a parent from our school is coming to this bar.

Lastly, the drink prices match our government-issued bank accounts.

Oh wait—that's five, which happens to match how many drinks I've had.

Guess I need another.

I raise my empty glass and motion toward the bartender, turn to my friends, and slur just a little. "You know what?"

"I don't think we want to know," says Maggie.

"I think those teacher conventions should have a sex-toy table," I say. "It would go over well in the educator world, don't you think?"

My friends are not impressed, but I really have thought this through. "Sex toys make people happy, and sometimes I think teachers are some of the most miserable human beings on the planet. A big purple dildo can go a long way for improving staff morale. Right?" I say as I look around for some confirmation on my plans for after retirement. "Sex sells," I say.

Mark says, "Speaking of sex, what happened to Jesus over the condom?"

That makes about five egregious Jesus incidents.

I react as though someone just cut me off in traffic, kicked my dog, and insulted my father, at the same time. "How many things can Jesus do before a real consequence happens? Everyone fucking plays pussyfoot with him so he doesn't throw down his stupid ass race card, when we've got five hundred more students of the same race throwing down their math assignments and social studies papers who we should be applauding and protecting from the Jesuses of the world."

"Daphne." My friend pats gently on my shoulder. "Maybe you should chill while you're on break," says Mark.

"Are you kidding? I am chill," I say. "You should see me when I'm really fired up."

The testing comment from hours ago still has me agitated.

"What's the big deal, Ms.?" someone said.

"It's boring, but who cares?" someone else said.

There were a lot of yeses after that, more students than not agreeing that testing should not be the bane of my career choice. But I was confused. I didn't understand why my students didn't complain, if we thought it would help, my friends and I would carry protest signs and march across Pearson's front lawn, our rally cry yelled from the rooftops, "Let us teach, not test!"

Then it occurred to me: Pearson is not interested in Abel or Gero or Manny or Destiny. They want their scores, they need their scores, and they want numbers, not humans, their desire to classify so strong they've taken the Department of Education hostage and held it for ransom.

What they do with those numbers I do not know, but I know one thing.

The state treats my students as though they are impoverished.

I treat them as if they have potential.

Six margaritas later and the Road to Graduation game board makes so much sense.

8

ABLE

I look up from the attendance because a third of my class are screaming, a third are laughing, and a third are yelling.

The math is probably inaccurate, but it's a chaotic second before I understand.

"Ms., look!"

It's a cockroach.

Not a tiny roach seeking retribution for the death of his family.

This one is the giant in your face I-don't-give-a-shit-you're-trying-to-teach kind.

The original class clown.

I take off my shoe and end his career.

My class screams again.

I take a picture with my cell phone and try to decide whether to send it to my colleagues or post it on social media.

I take a tissue, pick it up, and throw it away.

I tell the kids to get back to their books.

I pray they'll get back to their books.

But one student never looks up.

The public thinks of student readers as the book-nerd, full-on flashlight-under-the-covers, under-the-tree, at-the-bus-stop, on-the-bus, reading-books-until-the-day-I-die bookworm so engrossed, so stuck in a book, snot is running up and down inside the spine.

But that's not where I work.

I spend my day not with bookworms, but with bookthreads, baby worms unsuccessful with books. My job is to coax, prod, goad, cheer, push, shove, and beg my bookthreads to become bookworms.

If they hear what I say, do what I ask, and push themselves beyond the limits set by their potentially dangerous destinies, then just like the baby worm who takes a six-month journey from thread to worm, my students can do the same.

"Abel," I say. He looks up.

He points to his book, asks with his hand whether to bring it with him. I nod my head. He gets up and walks toward me, and as expected the lethargic Abel assumes the position, elbow on desk, head in hand, eyes slowly creeping their way to closed.

This is our first conversation since Weiss refused to let Abel leave her class to come to mine to read his poem.

"She hates kids," said Abel.

"I doubt that," I said.

"If you saw how she treats Manny, you'd think different," he said.

It was frustrating receiving the email declining my invitation for Abel to read, but I wrote a professional reply and then went home and took my teacher voodoo doll out of the drawer. A few select needles later, and I was over her.

Today is a different conversation, however. Abel has a copy of *The Absolutely True Diary of a Part-Time Indian*, and I wasn't the one who gave it to him.

"Where'd you get that?"

"The library," he said.

"The public library?"

"Yeah, I guess."

Yeah, I guess. Dude goes to the public library and checks out a book. Happens every day.

"Why?" I said.

"Manny said he liked it, and I knew you didn't have any more copies."

I try to picture this conversation, two guys with head nods, slide handshakes, and knuckle bumps.

"You like it?" asked Abel.

"It's cool," said Manny.

"Cool," said Abel, and then he went to the public library, like no big deal, all the guys in the neighborhood meeting at the library to read. Sure. Happens. Every. Day.

I ask him if he's ever been there.

"When I was like three," he says.

That makes more sense, the vast majority of parents excited about their toddlers and the alphabet and books and everything regarding reading, until life happens and school happens and then the shift of responsibility becomes the teachers' and the library is just a memory in a busy house with bills and dinner, bills and laundry, bills and bills.

"You're on ninety-seven? When did you get it?"

"Saturday, but I was busy, so I didn't get a chance to read."

"My bad. You're not funny; you're lazy."

Before the "Where I Am From" poem, he could look like he really was lazy, too lethargic to sit up straight or hold his head up high, but a boy like this would be hungry in a house full of food. "What's to eat?" filling his every thought.

I'm actually grateful Abel moved past *Tyrell* and *Bronxwood* and even *Perfect Chemistry*. Weeks ago Mark cured me of wanting to talk to any of my students about them, their R-rating terrorizing me and my teacher fantasies, my twenty-nine years of public school dedication ending with a police escort, me with my hands cuffed behind my back, me screaming, "It's not porn! It's not porn!"

"I'm going to get arrested," I said to Mark, "but it's not porn."

"Just keep telling yourself that," he said.

It was that same chill happy hour, just many, many drinks after the purple dildo comment.

"I had Hector when I first found out about those books. After he told me about the blow job page, I was freaking out, so when he was done with both of them, I asked him why I would give him those books."

"And?"

"He said to show him he has choices—that Tyrell's struggle is with his mother and father and accepting who they are, but in the end he realizes he doesn't have to be like either of them."

"And you're worried some nonreader is going to shut down your reading program, aren't you?"

Just 180 days a year for the last eight years—plenty of time to consider my life choices regarding my classroom library, books on my shelves capable of fueling a thousand book banners' wet dreams.

"It could happen. I'm basically giving my students measles to prevent measles."

"Is that what you call it?" he said, a smirk eclipsing his entire face.

"Why, smartass? What do you call it?"

"Admit it," he said. "You give out blow jobs to prevent blow jobs."

"You make me sound awful," I said.

"Are you kidding? You're a great teacher. I wish my teacher had handed out blow jobs. I would have started reading a long time ago."

Luckily, in the *True Diary of a Part-Time Indian*, the only person to get to third base is the protagonist with himself.

"How are you liking it so far?" I say to Abel, his lethargy still permeating his every pore except his lips, which, for the second time, seem to be smiling.

"I like it—I can relate."

Three and a half books inside a boy this size, this age, this many years swimming in melancholia. Maybe in fifty books I'll feel a little relief. For now, a third book means he's possibly gotten one shot of his five-shot inoculation series.

If Weiss is any indication of the rest of his day, then books are the only thing he's begun to care about.

"What are you doing over the break?" I say.

"Nothing," he says. "Probably just chilling with Jesus."

I ask where he lives. He describes a west-side neighborhood behind El Rio Golf Course. I've only driven through there, cars on blocks, broken windows, yards full of weeds, streets scattered with debris and empty beer cans.

"You know why I read?" I say. "Man Versus Self."

"What demons could an old lady like you possibly have?" he says.

"You'd be surprised," I say. "But we all have to learn to fight—who does Arnold have to fight?"

I don't wait for an answer. My patience with Jesus ended before it began, and I know Abel knows the answer. I picture him on his street. His arms are up, but his hands aren't fists, they're books. "Your biggest opponent will always be you," I say.

Jesus wants to bring you down; your neighborhood wants to keep you down, I don't say.

He's still smiling, no idea how terrified I am of Jesus's power over him.

"Okay, now get out of here. I need to call over your buddy Gero and about five other kids."

Abel laughs when he gets up. He knows Gero is still coasting, not reading like he should.

"Gero. Ms. Russell wants you," he says, still laughing.

"Aw, man," Gero says, "quit making fun of me—you're both mean."

Gero's defensive prepubescent voice is like the screech of a train attempting to stop, and it makes me laugh. "Oh, come on, Gero," I say. "I won't beat you up, I promise."

I laugh harder. Abel's giving me reason to laugh. It's an outlet for this smile on my face I can't quite stop. He's about to finish his fourth book, and he wants more.

Which makes it Gero's lucky day. For once, even though he's still not reading, I'm in too good of a mood to yell at him.

∽

"Merry Christmas," says Maggie, deadpan, slack-jawed, a hospital patient after eating a bowl of botulism for breakfast. "Ready for tomorrow?"

It's Monday morning. We're standing in the hallway, watching the kids move back and forth.

Pacheco refined our testing schedule into a neat and tidy four-day figgy-pudding fest.

They know it's testing week. We know it's testing week.

They know Thursday is their last day before Christmas.

We know Thursday is our last day before a meltdown of candy-striped proportions. Not only are we testing, but for the next four days, students start in their third-period class and stay there the entire morning, testing.

Note to self: Get Pacheco's address so I know where to send the Christmas card.

Testing protocols not covered in the manual:

1. Check purse for bottle of Xanax. Take half to one full tablet, depending on the makeup of your third period.

"You're excited about testing?"

"Did you know it's supposed to snow on Wednesday?"

Testing protocols also not covered in the manual:

2. Check purse for any Xanax that may have fallen into the bottom or stuck into any sneaky crevices. Take one tablet if the weather predicts snow. Take two if the snow begins to fall.

Abel, Manny, and Jesus are standing in a bad-boy huddle near the boys' restroom. Gero is outside of their circle. Not quite a bad boy, not quite a good one either.

If they looked like they were about to fight, I would walk toward them, lean over their shoulders, and intrude without a single word, just my presence to interfere with their drama.

I move closer in case I can overhear plans of ditching, marijuana toking, or better yet if it's Jesus, marijuana selling.

But they dissipate before I get too close. Disappointed, I move back toward Maggie.

"Damn," I say.

"They're up to something," she says.

"What pisses me off is that Jesus doesn't give two craps

about school, and without him, those other guys have at least a chance."

"I thought Manny was the problem."

"Manny doesn't have any power. Freaking Jesus has power, and those boys don't know he's not like the rest of them."

The final bell rings, and Maggie and I turn, reach out for our doors, and take the door stoppers off with our feet. We turn toward our rooms, soldiers before battle, Mother Teresa entering the casualty ward of the hospital.

I turn to my colleague. "You're Catholic, right? What's that cross thing? Will that help?"

"Dude," my friend says, "nothing can save you now."

For the layman imagine a sleepover with twenty-five kids, summer camp with thirty, CPR babysitting class with twenty-two, art class with fifty, the fund-raising car wash at the gas station with fifteen.

You are the only adult.

No one is coming to your rescue.

No breaks except to go potty.

Running from the building screaming is frowned upon.

But not unheard of...

Good luck.

Someone's going to need it.

"Okay, beautiful people, cell phones go in the box," I say. "Yes, cell phones in the box. Let's go over cell phones. First of all, they go in the box."

I walk around the room, box in hand, staring down the more hard core of my third-period crew but moving along casually as if I don't care about the consequences.

I don't linger and power struggle one-on-one.

I power struggle the whole class, walking, intimidating everyone as much as possible with my box, my real threats of inconvenience, because that's my only weapon against the phones. That, and a lunch period without social media, the equivalent to teenager hell.

The reason for the phone struggle is twofold. First of all, getting twenty-five cell phones out of young hands and into a box is more difficult than getting twenty-five, five-paragraph essays with perfect grammar and punctuation and appropriate citations into a basket.

Secondly, I don't believe in what I'm doing.

"If you are caught with your cell phone during this test, whether it's to check the time, a text from your mom, your dad, your uncle, your baby brother, your grandpa in the hospital, it doesn't matter. If I catch you with your phone during this test, we will go ahead and text your mom or your dad or your grandpa because they are the ones who are going to be picking up your phone after school or whenever they get around to it, but from the principal, not from me. So just put it in the box, and get it over with. You can't check it anyway."

The questions come flying—the but-whys and what-ifs and it's-so-irritating-to-begin-a-test-with-such-contentious-begin-nings, but we have to take the cell phones or we risk some kid on the phone and the drama that would ensue. The 911 call to the testing coordinator is not one I want to make.

Those teachers down in Georgia accused of cheating on the test?

Not me.

Don't get me wrong; I understand.

Some of my colleagues think this test reflects who they are, and it's not as though they're wrong, but they also aren't right.

I have these kids for one hour every day, sometimes less.

Let's do the math: In the period of the 180-day school

calendar, I have a student for 180 hours, give or take the flu, the dentist, the doctor, Disneyland.

Their parents and my colleagues have them for the other 4,140.

Don't give me too much credit. I'm neither that amazing nor that detrimental.

But what if a person's self-worth was dependent on a teenager's bubble sheet?

A fourth grader's?

Second grader's bubble sheet?

Don't judge unless you've held white chalk in your hand, written an objective or multiple objectives for the day, and then strove to meet those objectives with twenty-five or more children from varying backgrounds.

One year over winter break, a teacher shot herself in the head.

The only reason I don't erase a few and change a few answers is because I don't believe these tests are a reflection of me or my students.

If I did?

Give me one of those giant red erasers because this self-proclaimed Teacher of the Year has some bubbles to change!

Luckily that isn't me, and we haven't even started testing because I still don't have all the cell phones—plus everyone needs to go peepee and everyone needs a drink and everyone just broke the tip of their pencil and everyone needs to open their Gatorades and Powerades and cookies and Takis and gum packs, and we don't even know if the Wi-Fi is going to hold up.

And this is just the district test. Wait until it's the state test at the end of April.

Don't negate the weather either. It snows in Tucson about every ten years, so if it does snow this week, everyone is going to need to look out the window, stick their tongues out, and let the flakes fall gently into their mouths.

It's okay with me, and I'm not telling them about what is really going to happen. They don't need to know, while they wipe their noses and stare out into the cloudy sky, that the bubble-counting-test-checkers are going on an educational witch-hunt, and they're coming our way.

Four days of "Put your phones in the box."

"Do your best."

"Try your hardest."

"Every bubble counts."

Then, as an early Christmas present, we tell them all to go home for two weeks.

On Thursday afternoon we're instructed to follow the students out to the sidewalk and guide them gently, yet firmly, toward the buses. It takes the full force of all the cowboys, the wranglers, and the wrestlers to tell all the wild horses to get on home.

I'm busy yelling at some eighth-grade boys heading the opposite direction of the bus bay when I look down and see Destiny with a grin big enough to hang an ornament.

She holds out a bag. "I made it myself."

I picture food again, a pumpkin roll complete with warm cream cheese, dirty little fingers holding pumpkin-covered mixing beaters licked by a cute little tongue all covered with wiggly little germs attempting to render me helpless in bed for half of my winter break... but that doesn't stop me.

I reach into the bag.

My hand touches glass, and I pull out a skillfully layered candle with glitter near the wick.

"Destiny!" I say. "This is so awesome!"

"I thought you'd like it," she says.

"I do. It's perfect. How'd you do it?" I hold it out, turning it around in my hand, basking in the germ-free, preglow glow.

"My aunt helped me," she says.

This is the part of her life she didn't explain in her poem. Her mom lost custody of Destiny in the summer before school started.

"It's awesome," I say again. "Thank you."

I reach out and put my arm around her and gently squeeze her into me.

"You're welcome, Ms. Thanks for helping me read. I used to not like it, but now I do." She smiles that big Destiny smile. "You changed me."

"Aw, Destiny. You changed you. I was just standing here with the right book in my hand. You did all the work."

We hug again, and we tell each other to have nice Christmas breaks. That's what we say: "Have a nice break." Destiny doesn't know teachers don't have breaks. Sure, we aren't at school, but we take school home with us.

I turn toward my room when I hear, "What's up, Ms.?" I look up and see Jesus.

He side-eyes Maggie and tells her merry Christmas.

She says it back, sounding quite sincere.

"How'd you do that?" I say, after he's walked away.

"Oh, he's not so bad," she says.

I'd ask almost anyone what they are doing over the break, I'd tell them merry Christmas or have a great two weeks away from school, I'd give them a hug and say I'm looking forward to seeing them again in January, but not Jesus. He doesn't deserve my Christmas cheer.

Thoughts of Jesus do not worry me; it's his team of potentials.

Peer influence is the most powerful/underresearched factor in the success of a child, and two weeks of free time with Jesus as a playmate could make the strongest child throw a rock at a window, steal Takis at Circle K, or destroy some public property—a phone booth, a street sign...or worse.

"Hey, guys," I say to the three members of Jesus's social network following behind him.

Manny gives me a head nod, but Gero and Abel both tell me to have a nice break.

I tell them the same and act like I don't even see the book in Abel's hand.

"Make good choices," I say too. It's the best I can do under the circumstances—the contrast of the book and Abel's slimy sidekick make my insides hurt.

Two unsupervised weeks at home with parents at work is a lifetime.

Which reminds me, I should have taught a lesson on choices before vacation started. I use "vacation" loosely, though. There'll be no European trips over the break for my kids, no hitting the powdered slopes or Hawaiian beaches in their sunrises or sunsets.

"You finished with grades?" I say to Maggie.

"Hell, no," she says. "I'm going to be here all night in a locked room with the lights off so no one comes to talk to me."

The beginning of a teacher's winter break is akin to the empty nest of a parent; we clean, we meditate, we lament our past and plan our future.

"Drinks?" she says.

"Tomorrow? Sure. Let's get a crew together and slam a few." I laugh. "Were you there last time I drank?"

"I was."

"Okay, I promise, no more sex-toy talk."

"Can you even keep that promise?"

"No. I just want to make sure you'll be there."

Drinks sound good actually, right now preferably.

I'd pay money to get those first thirty-eight days back I missed with Abel. That's enough time to get two or three more books inside that boy. I don't know how many books it takes to do battle against someone like Jesus, but I do believe every page counts.

9

GRADING DAY

I was lured into the teaching profession by magical stories from my father of children overcoming insurmountable obstacles, the kid who couldn't read, the kid who didn't know his numbers, the kid who wouldn't speak, the student who became a teacher at the prison where his mother served her sentence...

I didn't realize there were hundreds and hundreds of children he never mentioned.

I have the same students in my classes.

There's Ian, who refuses to read books he likes and connect with characters who taunt him to read more.

I said, "It's as if you hate peanut butter and jelly sandwiches but you decide to eat them anyway, even though there is ham and cheese available," but it didn't change his mind.

There's Anna, who started reading the picture book *Lon PoPo* because the vocabulary in the simplest *Magic Tree House* was too challenging, and now, four months later, she's highlighting every word she doesn't know in *Drive By* so I can teach her those words and then she can read the book fluently on her own.

Mya just read *Drive By* with the same techniques I'm using with Anna.

If Mya's connections were deep enough and her new vocabulary is strong enough, she'll be able to tackle her next book with newfound confidence.

Seleste said she'd never read, but she finished *Tyrell* in a semester. She never took it home, but she was diligent when reading in class.

Izac read three out of the *Bluford High* series—*Tears of the Tiger, True Diary, Tyrell, Bronxwood, The Skin I'm In,* and *Homeboyz.*

Now, along with a hundred or so more, I have to assign all these children a single alphabet letter to represent their growth in reading over the last five months.

May I suggest a translation of Aramaic text into modern-day English by a teenage Buddhist Monk?

It may be a more accurate representation.

But I have no choice. I must manage to differentiate my teaching as well as the way I assign grades while still following an educationally justifiable series of alphabet letters.

Essentially, if a student follows my two rules every day, then she will receive a passing grade.

1. Read all the words.
2. Make connections to the words.

When a student can't answer my questions about a book, I ask which rule she is breaking. They're posted on the back wall, so the child will turn around, read the two rules, look back at me, and say, "I'm skipping words," or, "I'm not making enough connections," and then we talk about whether she should change books or come up with a plan when the text gets harder or she doesn't understand what's being said.

The process takes anywhere from one day to half a year.

It's beautiful really, unless it doesn't work.

Gero still cannot follow my two rules.

It's only two rules.

After four tries on his own, I picked a book for him.

I checked to see if he knew the most difficult words in chapter one.

He did.

The book is about a boy who lives with his mother and sister.

Gero lives with his mother and sister.

He can read the words, he can make the connections, but he's not moving forward at a pace that makes me happy. In the end it is about me, right?

What he doesn't know is I've been sweet like a chocolate bar on a Tucson summer day, but if he's not careful, I may start trying harder, melting all over his hands.

After the break I'll say, "Hey, Gero? How 'bout you read a chapter a day, or you get a detention that day, every day. Cool?"

"Cool," he'll say, but he won't mean it, and I will be counting exactly how many after-school detentions it will take to make Gero read. If necessary I'll use all ninety.

But that's next semester. For now, in my grade book, I give him zero out of fifty for the assignment called Second Quarter Book. It doesn't kill his grade, but it gives him a C when he would have had a B, possibly an A. I click the teacher comment that says, "Not working to potential," and I cross my fingers someone at home cares enough to put at least one piece of coal in his stocking.

As for Abel's grade, I have to look through his grades in his other classes before deciding.

Yes, it's probably illegal. Yes, I do it anyway.

He's still failing two *core* classes, still trying to be the Tallest Boy on Earth at the middle school version of a sideshow. I give him a D.

Manny gets an F because the only productive thing he's done is read for me, but I never made the deal with him I made with Abel. I click the "Shows improvement," teacher comment for him and laugh at the thought of Weiss seeing the F and "improvement" together.

Eventually exhaustion over the least interesting of my professional duties overcomes me, and I check my email as a distraction.

I'm in a group email from the counselor that says Diego is coming back and I have him again.

I check the email list and note the monitor he had pushed wasn't included.

I stop grading, log off my computer, and stand up.

Christmas break?

Is that some sort of joke?

A teacher's break is not much different than one night in the life of Ebenezer Scrooge—he and I with a great deal to talk about over eggnog and red-and-white-striped candy canes, so much regret.

I wish I would have pushed a few kids harder, a few softer, a few I feel slipped right through the cracks in my room between Manny, Destiny, and the tiny cockroaches now in a permanent slumber in my cabinets.

I won't be at work after tomorrow, but next week I'll see an ex-student at the mall or the movies or a restaurant and I'll say hi and we'll hug and I'll win the ex-Teacher of the Year award if I remember the name of the child who now embodies this woman with the baby or this man with the beard. I'll think about who they were when they were thirteen and I'll convey my feelings from ten and twenty years before when this grown man was a little kid in a class surrounded by twenty-five more just like him, but in that moment I will cull him back, back into the restaurant or bar if it's been a while, and we'll laugh about what he was like and he'll remember me a bit nicer than I feel because I feel a little nicer over winter break.

And this is just one of my days off.

On another day I'll see a student I don't remember as fondly, and I'll still remember something good about him and say something nice. In ten years even Jesus will get a tiny slice of Christmas cheer.

But for the first time in a few months, I'm actually not thinking about the damage Jesus may inflict on Abel and the boys. Oh no, the potential of the return of Hurricane Diego has eclipsed any worries about what Jesus may do in his neighborhood over the next two weeks.

I'm worried about what Diego could do in my classroom when two weeks are over.

If I don't meet people for drinks tomorrow, I'm going to have to go to the gym.

Even without being contained in a forty-by-forty space every day, it's certain now, no doubt about it: my Christmas break does not include a chance for me to chill.

10

WHITE FLAGS

My stepmother, retired teacher, thirteen years free and clear of any classroom obligations, still suffers teachers' chalkboard nightmares.

"I dreamed I was being evaluated by the entire school board," she says over dinner. "They're faceless, but it's them, all of them in the back of the room, taking notes. Their pens writing I don't know what."

My parents have two traditions since retiring from the public school system: margaritas on the beach on August 1 and an RV tour de los casinos January 1.

This is their idea of a good time, while the rest of us crawl our way back into classrooms.

They leave in the morning.

"Can you pass the potatoes?" I say to my dad.

My childhood house is still home to my parents, a 1960's ranch style on the outside, upgraded southwest Arizona décor on the inside, Kokopellis adorning the entertainment center encasing the thirty-inch television.

"I had no objective on the board, no lesson plans on my desk," says the only mom I know. "The kids are all running around the room, chasing each other and throwing things, while I stand at the pencil sharpener trying to sharpen just one pencil. I keep turning the handle over and over again and the pencil just gets smaller and smaller but it won't sharpen."

"That actually sounds like the sharpener in my room," I say.

The two thousand pencils our principal bought can't be sharpened in the pencil sharpeners bolted down to our countertops in our rooms. I guess Pacheco was right when he held up the pencil in the staff meeting and publicly shamed us for not acknowledging its technological advancement. It's at least as advanced as our Wi-Fi capabilities.

Mom and I are commiserating over her past drama and my present drama when my dad interrupts. "I ever tell you about that girl I had? I don't think she even knew the letters of the alphabet when I got her—"

"I don't know, maybe—probably," I say.

He pulls out his deep southern drawl and sets it down right next to the Mississippi River. "I gave her a copy of *Stone Fox* and had her read that first page o'er and o'er again until she could picture it in her head—sick grandpa, boy trying to take care of 'im—"

"Yeah?"

"Was reading *Old Yeller* by the end of the year—she's a nurse now—just had a baby and invited me to the shower."

Pop's version of the One-Up Club.

I debate between all my stories of Abel.

There's the one when Abel said he was going to give *True Diary* to his nephew.

"The one in seventh grade?" I asked, grateful the nephew would already have one book inside him before he arrived at my room next year, glad Tio Abel could see the potential of his influence.

Then I remembered.

I'm retiring in five months.

I think of telling Pop the one where, in the middle of a completely silent room of silent reading, Abel put his hand at the bottom of *Bronxwood*, held his place, turned to Gero next to him, and said, "You really are an idiot. This one is better than the first," then turned back to his book and finished.

Then there's the time Abel read *Perfect Chemistry* and faced the entire class from his perch on my stool, his head not resting in his palm this time, his eyes wide open and ready, everything about him in such contrast to his usual sleepy-sloth look.

The girls brought the fire.

"What happened to Paco?" said someone, taunting him, not even secretly hoping he couldn't answer.

"How did Brittany change?" said someone else, smiling, obviously teasing, clearly heckling Abel under her breath.

"What was Brittany's Man Versus Self struggle?"

"Who won the fight?"

"How did it end?"

They tried to trip him up, get him to get one answer wrong, but he never hesitated, never even skipped a step. After a few minutes, the girls gave up.

"He read it," someone said.

"Yeah, he read it," someone else agreed.

I knew he'd read it before the bombardment began, but the moment made Abel part of my sales team for the *Perfect Chemistry* series, and now the boys would take it more seriously and consider adding one to their personal library list.

A few weeks later, he had *True Diary* in his hand, and we talked about what he should read over the break. I suggested *Always Running* by Luis Rodriguez.

"But what about the other books in that *Chemistry* series?" he said.

I told him I had enough copies. "It's up to you," I said.

"Well, what's it about?"

This moment reminded me that I'd like to email those researchers who came up with fifteen-hundred-decisions-a-day estimate.

More like fifteen hundred an hour.

Fifty possible scenarios of what to say pass through my mind.

"Is it safe to go out in your neighborhood at night?" I said.

"No, not really. Why?"

"Do you go out at night anyway?"

"Yeah. Why?"

I told him *Always Running* is about a guy who had to make a lot of choices, most likely many of the same Abel has to make.

This is the story I choose to tell my dad.

"That's a worthy goal," he says. "Helping a guy make some good choices—how's everything else going?"

He wants to know about my principal, about the parents, anything about my school that will remind him of his teaching days, but he likes the success stories, and my mind is consumed with failures right now.

I don't tell him how Diego is about to come back and I question whether or not I can keep his headphones and hoodie off without engaging in a power struggle.

I don't want to tell him how Maria is dating a seventh grader and how the boy isn't worth the dirt on the bottom of Maria's shoe, but she ignores all my attempts to break them up.

Nor do I drone on about the lack of Band-Aids in the nurse's office or the lack of toilet paper in the bathroom or the crappy pencils and crappy internet or the gum-stained concrete or about the cockroach festival that just went down for the last two weeks with no one there to scare the brats back into hiding.

I say nothing about the rumors Destiny's mom will probably get back the custody she lost so many months ago. And I definitely don't tell him I can't get Gero to read because I really can't get Gero to read, and three thousand copies of *Stone Fox* aren't going to get Gero to read.

I answer him though; it would be rude otherwise.

"Not much," I say. "Not much."

The next morning I enter Mission Heights as my last first day of the second semester. In celebration I text Mark: "Two things: It's not porn, and I hate you."

My keys are in the door when he texts back. "#blwjbpusher."

I text, "#jerkface," but it's lame compared to his hashtag, so before pressing *send*, I copy and paste the word over and over again until I know my text will fill his screen.

Then I send a single smiley face emoji and start my school day by putting down my things and heading straight for the cafeteria, where the school monitor will be stationed.

The first semester and the second semester are both ninety days long, but that is where their similarities end. The first half of the year is like a gentle hike around the lake with an occasional tiny jaunt out into the woods and back. The second half is like climbing Mount Everest naked with one liter of water and a granola bar.

I'm exaggerating.

I should have said, "naked except for socks and boots."

Part two of the school year is difficult enough without having the boy who pushed you showing back up at school, unannounced. Letting the monitor know Diego will be walking into the cafeteria any moment now in order to get his two-pancake allotment with a skinny piece of sausage on the side is not in my job description, but it is obviously the right thing to do.

"Nope," she says.

I repeat my question. "Pacheco didn't email you and tell you Diego would be here today?"

"He did not," says the ex–LA gang member, a picture of a cross tattooed on one forearm, a picture of a cholo and his chola on a tricked-out chopper on the other. She doesn't have a visible teardrop tattoo, but there's an underlying bloodline that states, "Cross me, and I'll shank you."

"That little boy pushing me was no big thing," she says, "but someone sure should have told me he was coming back."

We're friendly, always friendly. We both speak Child, and that's where most of our conversations lie, but not today. Today I want her to know I also have her back, if not in the streets, definitely here at work, where we should feel safe, and I can tell by her demeanor that her warrior pose isn't working. Her south-side old-school swagger just skipped a step.

"So, just to clarify, the fourteen-year-old pushing you didn't hurt at all, but the admin not telling you about his return does?"

"Yep, it sure does. It hurts a lot actually."

I email everyone on the original pre-Christmas Diego email and add a few more key people: the community representative, the other two counselors, the principal and vice principal, the school nurse, and the monitor.

I ask if we could talk about a plan. "Diego had some extreme behaviors before he was asked to leave, and maybe we could come to a consensus on our expectations for him."

I don't go into details about teachers' complaints of Diego's defiant behavior, issues with day-to-day compliance—his final stand before the incident with the monitor was refusing to let the monitor search his bag.

Within an hour Pacheco writes back. "We went over our expectations with him and made it clear what we need from him as far as behavior is concerned, and he seemed okay with everything we said."

He added, "We're giving Diego a fresh start."

Fresh start.

Funny he should say that. There's a rumor Pacheco dated Diego's mom back in high school. As a distraction to my obsession, I'm grateful when my second period of the day saunters their way into my room.

I'm relieved they all arrive.

Even Manny seems to pay a special visit on this first day back to school.

What's up and knuckle bumps as they pass, a couple hugs and one *hey.*

"Hey," Abel says back.

I take attendance, do my normal thing, nothing on my radar, nothing I want to do, just thinking about a victim, someone who may have lain a little too low last semester and not read enough...

Then I see Gero is holding a book.

What?

Wait.

What?

Abel is leaning over, pointing, smiling, and laughing just enough to let me know we both know something Gero does not.

Giving Gero *True Diary* never occurred to me. With a psychologist's diagnosis of dyslexia, a doctor's diagnosis of ADHD, and my own diagnosis of apple-and-the-tree syndrome, I'd given up believing he could read enough of the words of any book in order to make connections.

When I call him over, he sits hesitantly on the stool. He looks worried, but he should be worried. He's never once been successful on this stool.

"Read that page," I say.

"Ms.," he says, "this ain't a good page to read."

I laugh. Even his answer gives me hope. I know exactly what page seduced him into reading.

"Well, why were you even on that page?"

"Abel told me to read it."

"You understood that whole page?" I say.

He smiles. "Yes, Ms., but don't ask me no questions about it. That's embarrassing."

This may be my most favorite blackmail yet.

"Since I know you can read that page, why don't we go ahead and make a deal—you read that whole book, and I won't tell your mother what page you love so much."

"Ms.," he said. "You wouldn't."

"Are you sure about that?"

No matter what he says, Gero can never be 100 percent sure Ms. Russell won't tell Mrs. Sanchez that her cute little son loves himself some text about masturbation.

"A'ight, Ms., I'll read it—but please don't be calling my mom—she'd beat me with her chankla."

He doesn't know, but it's possible I'd pay money to watch that happen.

When I finish with Gero, I call over Manny. His attendance is so erratic, I have to call him over. He may never come back.

When he takes his spot on the stool, a white bandana hangs behind him. I grab it from his pocket and place it on his lap.

I suppose I should be happy. He is here in my class on my stool, the first day after Christmas break after an extended vacation, a cruise perhaps, a cross-country road trip possibly, or a visit to all the national parks and amusement parks from here to New York, maybe.

Or not.

To those lab coat researchers and their tombstone colleagues, I have another check box for you.

"Ms.? Why'd you do that?" Manny says.

"You know why," I say.

"It's just a bandana."

I'm a suicide counselor with a potential jumper, one foot dangling over the edge.

"You have a sister, don't you?"

"Two. Why?"

It's just that I know he has family members in gangs, and now he has his white bandana. I need him to know his influence matters, that what he does his sisters will follow.

I want to comment on the white bandana too, ask him if he knows what waving the white flag used to mean, what it means to other people, and then I want to rip that symbol of warfare and territory out of his pocket for good, but I know that's not how this goes.

"Where are you in your book?" I say. He opens it, shows me the place where he dog-eared the page. "Two hundred ten, sweet. I can't wait to talk to you about it when you finish. Why don't you just go back to your seat and see how much more you can read before class is over?"

He says, "All right, Ms.," as he slips off my stool and heads for his desk.

"Here," I say. I hand the bandana back to him. "Put it in your backpack, not your pocket."

I question giving the bandana back, question what I didn't say, question how I should have told him how girls are initiated in gangs.

But I know he knows.

My students' lives are fragile, and they should never be placated with a candy coating, yet I just smothered our conversation with chocolate icing and whipped topping and added some tiny sprinkles on top.

Sometimes this job…

Two classes later and I need a nap, but I head toward the library.

"Fresh start?" the community representative says to me at lunch in her office. "What the hell is a fresh start? You never said he wasn't going to have a fresh start—you said you wanted to meet. Why doesn't Pacheco want to meet?"

"I have no idea," I say.

Michelle is my lunch buddy partly because she never steals my lunch, but mostly because she doesn't trash talk our students.

Her office is located inside the library. We keep the door shut for the sake of the library visitors.

"Shoulda figured out a way to make it Pacheco's idea," she adds.

"Pete does like control, doesn't he?" I say.

As I get up to head to class, Michelle's phone rings, and she holds up her finger, telling me to wait. "Mission Heights Middle School, Mrs. T. speaking. Can I help you?"

I wait to see if I know who's calling her, acknowledgement that it's Maggie or Mark or someone else we can heckle and harass, but she reaches for the mouse on her computer and says, "I'd be happy to look that up for you—what is your child's name?"

She isn't sarcastic, but she isn't exactly friendly, and I wonder what is being said on the other side.

"Sir, now just wait a minute, I am checking—it looks as though—sir? Sir? There is no need to curse at me—no I am not the teacher—I am trying to see if Abel was here during third period—oh no, there is no need to yell—thank you, sir, I hope you do call our principal."

She looks at me and hangs up the phone. "He hung up," she says.

"Was that Abel Cazares's dad?"

"Yeah."

"I love that kid."

"I don't think you'd love his dad."

"I don't think he even lives with his dad," I say.

By the time fifth period rolls around, I have so much disgust with Pacheco and so much hope for Gero that I risk everything by calling over Diego as soon as class begins.

Just like couples, students have honeymoon stages. The beginning of the school is a week or so long with "yes, ma'ams" and "no, ma'ams," sweet talk and quiet talk, walking without the running.

After a week?

It's as if someone stole all the fences from the zoo.

Diego could last about a week in his honeymoon stage, but I won't.

"Hey," I say.

"Hey," he says, his hair pushed back, hoodie on, and earphones in his ears.

"You're back." I use my hand to subtly suggest he slide down his hoodie and take out his earbuds.

"I'm back," he says, and he complies with my request, but we both know it's not permanent. The second he walks away, he will return them both.

Fresh starts do nothing to curb habitual behavior.

I consider making a statement about the hoodie and headphones, an ultimatum possibly, a threat of some sort.

Instead I grab a copy of *Tyrell* from my desk and set it in front of him. "You didn't read for me last time you were here," I say.

He starts to make excuses, but I'm not listening.

"You're here now, and you're going to read—no choice—no way out."

"What's it about anyway?" he says.

"Choices," I say.

Diego is not like any of my other students. He wasn't the first time around, and he's not now. Hoodies and headphones are about control, and for a child to refuse compliance over two overt rules and subject himself to the consequences of breaking those rules means his life is completely unmanageable.

The problem is, today they aren't an issue but tomorrow they may be and Diego and I never had enough time to establish a relationship and now I'm out of time.

I add, "If you read for me, I'll let you do other teachers' work, but I'm serious—you have to read for me."

I don't know if he's listening or if he's understanding at all, but I don't care. I'm going to try anyway.

"What if I don't like it?"

"You're reading it anyway."

"I thought it was about choices," he says.

"The book is," I say. "I'm not."

Diego smiles at my joke. We may not have a relationship, but we have an understanding, and for a first meeting, a joke is more than reasonable. Everyone else, however, is on my hit list. I'm in grade-checking mood, and may the book gods help the child who didn't read for me and has failing grades when I'm in this mood. I start to call over every single student who slid past my wrath last semester.

Diego needs to see I take no prisoners when I teach, and despite my conversations being inaudible to the rest of the class, it is still apparent it's not fun time at Ms. Russell's desk.

"How'd it go?" says Maggie as we swing our doors open for the last bell of the day. "My kids seemed a little cray-cray."

"Ms.," says Destiny, right under me, a head full of blue hair, sunglasses pushing the blue back, fake eyelashes weighing down her eyelids, aging her in a way that makes me uncomfortable.

"Hey, check it out," I say as I touch a strand.

"My mom did it," she says. She flips her hair back and forth to make sure I see the color, but all I can see are the eyelashes.

Destiny Conrad, proof child protective services may be the only government office more treacherous than the office of education.

"Wow!" I say, and I smile.

I'm an actor, after all. The Academy would call if they knew I existed.

"I like the look with the glasses," I say. "But you can't wear them in class."

"I know, Ms."

I look at her and remember she wasn't in class. "Where were you?"

"My mom was coloring my hair," she says.

She's starts talking more, telling me how long it took, how she's loving the *Harry Potter* series and she's up to book four, how she doesn't like the generic Froot Loops her mother buys.

"Is she picking you up?" I say as I fantasize a little fight between me and mamacita. It would be clean and all, no need to call the authorities.

I grab my door, flip up the doorstop. I look at Maggie while she does the same.

No words this time; we're just going to go in our rooms and hide.

This is just what we do.

We're like the ironworkers who maintain the Golden Gate Bridge and man the suicide crisis line, regular guys trained to make repairs and keep the safety features intact. When there's a potential jumper, these are the ones called, not social workers or police officers with negotiation strategies, just ironworkers who know how to negotiate the dangers of the bridge.

I read about one of these guys with a 6 percent mortality rate. He had to quit taking phone calls for over a year after the last one jumped.

I felt the same when Manny walked past just moments ago, the white cotton square hanging loosely again from his back pocket as he and Jesus high five in the middle of the hallway.

I could mourn Manny. I could whine and go home and chug a bottle of wine and take off tomorrow, but I can't.

I don't have 180 days anymore.

When I walk up the steps tomorrow and make my way to room 111, I'll only have 89.

11

WADDLE TECH

Maybe it's because teenagers aren't supposed to be awake and functioning at nine thirty in the morning, maybe the cold air outside and the warm air inside were natural sedatives for a group of people more likely to be in the mosh pit of a concert than in a seat in the stands, but my note from the substitute teacher for second period said they were fine.

I ask Abel to run an errand.

"Just a sec," he says, and proceeds to put his backpack on his desk.

"What are you doing?" I say.

He opens his bag and pulls out a second pair of shoes.

"Can't crease 'em, Ms.," he says.

I watch carefully as he takes off his clean white shoes one at a time. He puts on his obviously older shoes and ties them.

"I don't understand," I say as he gets up and walks toward me.

"Can't crease my shoes," he says again, with an exaggerated accent of some kind of cool he typically doesn't speak.

"You crease them when you walk?" I say.

I get it now. If he bends his feet when he walks, then the tops of his shoes get creases in them.

"I can resell them," he says as he waddles out the door with the message I wrote to the monitor asking if she can watch my class while I run to the restroom. I'd like to say I could just use the school phone and then someone would radio a monitor, but that's not how this works. Nobody at Mission Heights Middle School actually answers the phone.

Once I asked our office secretary what the most common complaint she'd ever heard was. She told me parents always complain no one answers the phone.

"While you're on the phone with a parent, the parent tells you no one answers the phone?" I said.

"Yep," she said.

Which means waddling Abel is the fastest form of technology available for my bladder issue.

Not to miss a second of teaching, I tell the kids to make sure they have paper and a pencil by the time I get back. Occasionally I'm obsessed with a lesson, and today is one of those days.

Yesterday I took the day off to get an updated physical and my semiannual dental cleaning. I'm eight months away from losing my fairly good insurance, so I need to take advantage before it's too late.

Early on in my career, I had an engineer friend I was trying to tell about the difficulties of taking a day off from work. He laughed and said it's hard for everybody. "Whenever you come back, there's always shit that didn't get done," he said.

Shit that didn't get done.

If only.

First of all it takes two hours to take off eight hours from teaching. In its most simplistic form, something has to be written for a stranger to read and then to implement with twenty-five to thirty children the stranger has never met. If it's a middle school or high school, this event is repeated five to six times for an hour at a time.

Elementary school?

This lesson plan must be written in order to safely entertain twenty-five to thirty-five tiny children for seven and a half hours.

What could go wrong?

Apparently, with second period, nothing. The rest of the day, however, is a completely different story.

Second period is getting off easy. I'm in a good mood, no need for punishment with these people, just an old-fashioned lesson that has me obsessed.

"Adults shouldn't have to pee this way," I say to the monitor when I return. "Our bathroom breaks should be more dignified."

"At least you have a one-holer," he says. "The boys' bathroom here doesn't even have doors."

I could talk about the indecency of that statement, but I must get back to my lesson. As I walk through my door, I announce, "I was serious about the pencils, people."

Immediately five kids get up and head toward my desk.

"Are you serious? You had the whole time I was gone to get ready."

Pencils.

Last year Jesus broke off my bolted-down sharpener when my back was turned.

"Oh, sorry, Ms.," he said, entire black sharpener in his hand, an insincere apology oozing from his lips.

I bought a twenty-dollar sharpener guaranteed to sharpen any pencil on the planet.

Maybe they really meant "planet" and not a classroom where kids actually sharpen pencils.

I've already invested in two extra blades.

My desk is a merry-go-round, five kids right now, later ten more, then about twelve, another ten, then eleven, ending with about seven to fifteen, depending on the weather. Literally.

Ms., I need a pencil, a Band-Aid, markers, a pass to the library, to the bathroom, to the nurse, to the office, to the counselor.

Can I borrow your scissors?

A compass?

A ruler?

A calculator?

Do you have a Kleenex?

"Ms., how was your weekend?" says Gero.

"Good," I say, skeptical, suspicious. "How was yours?"

"I went to the carnival. Did you go? It was cool."

"Those street-corner carnivals scare me. One loose screw and you're dead. What do you want?" I say.

"A pencil," he says.

I contemplate my futuristic job opportunities, none of which involve carney workers, school supplies, or the supervision of children in a confined space where corporal punishment is frowned upon...

"Ms.," says Destiny, "did Mr. B. talk to you about me?"

He hasn't, I'm fairly certain, but while I'm still thinking of ways to hide Gero's body, Destiny spins the handle of my million-dollar sharpener. Resisting the temptation to throw it, I take it from her hands instead and set it back down gently on my desk.

"No, sweetie, he hasn't, but I'll ask him about you and see what's up, but right now I have to teach."

And I do; I'm not just saying this.

"I think my mom's going to have me arrested today," she says. "Oh, and can I go to see Mrs. T.?"

My mouth is open, but no words come out.

"I need to ask her for some pipe cleaners for my science project," she says.

"Sure," I say, a firefighter on his third fire of the day, a police officer's second domestic violence call in an hour, a tour bus pulled up to a breakfast joint with one waitress and one cook. "Just go. You don't need a pass," I add.

Destiny walks out whistling. I don't know what she means by the arrest or even the pipe cleaners, but I still have my idea about teaching an actual lesson today, no matter what happens.

I look up at the clock.

I only have thirty minutes.

"Okay, people. I'm passing out a paper, and we're going to read the first paragraph together, but there's something I need to talk about first—"

The phone rings. It's the registrar calling to check out a student.

The counselor walks into the room, points at Abel, and motions him over.

"Ms., have we had lunch yet?" is yelled from the back of the room.

I imagine what a hot tub may feel like, what Club Med would look like. I picture pulling the fire alarm and ponder the results of such a lapse in judgment.

But I continue forward and tell the kids about how words are used to persuade.

"Like 'bandwagon,'" someone says.

"Yes, like 'bandwagon,'" I say. "The true idea with words, not the PG version, but the R-rated, what's-really-happening version, is that words are used to persuade groups of people to think alike—"

Three students raise their hands, but I don't call on them. "Just wait," I say, and then someone yells out, "Like Super Bowl American car ads?" and I acknowledge her because she's right and I'm just not that good at classroom management.

"Yes, we already talked about that, how a person can be a better American by driving a Chevy or a Ford, how patriotic it used to be to drink Budweiser."

Like a TV show, I try to keep going and keep them entertained because I cannot afford one more commercial interruption or I'm going to crack.

"And now we're going to talk about something from history, something that I can show you pretty easily without any teachers getting upset that I'm teaching an alternative history, because I'm not. I'm teaching you how to read history."

Years ago a colleague introduced me to *Lies My Teacher Told Me*, and I've been trying to figure out how to teach the concepts James Loewen pushed in his epic outcry over biased history books ever since.

"First of all, let me ask you all this: if there is a fight, who tells the story?"

"The winner," someone says.

"Yes, the winner," I say. "And what if I were the winner of the fight, but I had bullied the kid all year? Would I tell you about the bullying?"

A unison of nos.

"Guess what version this is?" I ask.

"The winner" is repeated by multiple people.

"Yes, the winner. Let's take a look at the first paragraph," I say.

We read together, identify words together. The vocabulary is simple, no word too difficult for my eighth-grade readers, most of whom are on their fourth and fifth books of the year.

What is complicated for me, for them, for anyone, is what is actually being said behind the words, the subversion of racism so much more complicated than the flag-waving KKK grand master.

"We're going to make a T-chart with the vocabulary describing the US Army on one side and the Navajo people on the other. Let's start with 'awe.' Who is in awe?"

We talk through the implication that the Navajo people were simple and would think the army's Fort Defiance to be something of wonder.

"Now let's look at 'warriors.' What does 'warrior' mean to us?"

"Violence," someone says.

"Fighting," someone else says.

"Weapons," someone says.

"What about 'army?'" I say. "What does 'army' mean to us?"

"Protection," someone says.

"Anything else?" I say.

No one says a word.

The army protects and warriors attack.

Got it.

The list is long on both sides, but yet one-sided.

"Why are all the negative words on the Navajo side?" someone asks.

"Why do you think?" I ask.

We go through what would have happened. Settlers travel across North America, find places to stop, it's in Navajo territory, the army puts the Navajo people on reservations and tells them to stay there.

According to the vocabulary, the Navajo raided, attacked, threatened.

The United States were neighbors. They were involved only

in "small skirmishes," and instead of killing people, they "beat them off."

Two hours after this lesson, I'm standing in front of my seventh-grade class.

Much research confirms the twelve-to-thirteen-year-old brain is in the least stable transition of its life.

I knew a teacher who mapped out her entire school year with the same lesson plans every single year for nearly twenty years. August meant an apple-themed beginning with butcher-paper trees and construction-paper cutouts of the fruit of the month.

I could never make that happen. Differentiating in my class means a student points out an inability to see the irony in her book, and I teach a lesson on irony. A student struggles with making connections with her book, and I help her create a bookmark map of connections she maintains throughout the duration of the book. A student cannot quite read *Drive By*, and I help her highlight trouble words and teach her the words, and then she reads the chapters one at a time independently, making connections as she reads.

It's complicated, but I have a technique for every kind of reader, and I can use a school library to teach every one.

Except on days like today.

Today we read one essay together as a class. While my second period committed no crimes against humanity, my fourth period was referred to by the sub as "a destructive force of nature."

It will take me three days to fix the damage that's been done.

I'm not a planner. I really couldn't do an apple-themed month. Ever. Much less redo the same plans every year. I swear I would start sniffing chalk within the first hour of year two.

But when I'm disappointed in behavior, disillusioned

by apathy, disgusted by the complete disregard for another human's life, I pull out one lesson inspired by the movie *Coach Carter* and the quote by Marianne Williamson.

With Mr. Martinez's sub note in my hand, I sat in my cushy office chair and thought about my options:

1. Seating chart for everyone
2. Seating chart for people with names written down
3. Have all students participate in a tell-all, with double punishment for the purposeful exclusion of personal behavior
4. Teach the *Deepest Fear* lesson

Before I took Tuesday off, I told all my classes, "I don't care how mean or nasty or inflexible or confused the sub is when I take off for a day or two, so let me make it very clear: I don't want to see your name written down."

"But what if it's for a good reason?" someone asked.

"What if he's mean?" someone else asked.

"I don't care," I said, and then, in each class, I pointed to someone who never does anything wrong, and I added, "Okay, if Maria gets her name written down, then I will ignore the sub note."

There's always a collective groan after that, everyone knowing what no one will admit: self-control is possible in every situation and expected in this one.

Some classes weren't so bad, the biological teenage morning lethargy working in favor of the substitute teacher, but by the afternoon, lethargy had transformed into a collective conscience of class coughing, random whistling, name changing, paper-wad flying, and under-the-breath barking. Rather than pinpoint every scene, I gave after-school detentions for students with their names written down, and then I started the ultimate life lesson through text, Man Versus Self, the entire reason behind the quote.

I print enough copies and steel myself for the excuses.

"But, Ms., that lady was rude."

And, "Ms., she sent me out for no reason…"

I attacked every excuse mercilessly.

"So, why couldn't you just sit there? Why did you have to get out of your seat? Should we call your mom and explain the situation? You can tell her how I should expect less of you than all my other students, right? And then I'll get on the phone, and she'll yell at me for having the audacity to assume you could behave without a babysitter and—"

Inevitably, at this point, someone whispers, "Dude, shut up and say you're sorry—she's not going to stop until you do."

It's somewhat of a buzz kill, those kids who know me all too well, but it does stop me and helps me regain focus.

"Now take out the text *Our Deepest Fear* and tell me why in the world your crazy teacher would give you this. Why would she expect more from you? Better from you? Everything from you?"

In every class where the sub note was less than favorable, I ask, "'When I let my light shine, I unconsciously allow others to do the same.' What does that mean?"

I show the clip of the basketball player repeating the speech in the *Coach Carter* movie. Fictional or factual, Coach Carter and I want the same.

More.

Parents want more.

Teachers want more.

El Grupo de los Pobrecitos?

I'm not so sure.

I address Diego in the hallway before his class begins, before I slap a copy of *Our Deepest Fear* into his hand.

"I heard you left," I say.

"I went to Pacheco," he says.

"Did the sub tell you to go to Pacheco?"

"No."

In real life normal kids need three words. "Hey, no hoods." Kids like Diego need a well-thought-out battle plan with charts, maps, diversionary tactics, and strategizing. And now that he gained power by being consoled by Pacheco, I have two problems.

It's not just a matter of compliance; it's a matter of power. Diego has none of his own, so he's trying to take mine, using the principal. A student like Diego will do whatever it takes to win.

What he doesn't know is, I'm on his side too. I had to figure out how to give him power without losing my own.

Complicated, yes, but not impossible.

Luckily, I went to school for this.

Before Diego's class, instead of monitoring the crazies in the hallway with Maggie, I write on the blank chalkboard in the back of the room in giant bold letters: "When the final bell rings, your hoods will be down and your headphones off or you will put them on my desk. Refusal to comply will result in an after-school detention with Mark."

The first student in the room says, "What's that?"

"A rule in bold letters," I say.

"Cool," he says.

The second person in the room is Diego. I watch him read the words on the board. He turns to me. "What if I don't go to the detention?" he says.

"You have to deal with Mark," I say, fingers crossed behind my back, hopeful the Bounty Hunter nickname is enough to detour Diego from choosing his hoodie-filled destiny.

The bell rings and I read the rule out loud while everyone looks back and follows along. "That means now," I say, "and tomorrow that means before the final bell rings."

A couple kids take off their hoodies. They would have anyway, but those are the kids who will mindlessly flip their hoodies back up. Diego isn't mindless.

Tomorrow one of those kids will flip the hood back up, and I will have no choice but to assign him a detention.

In this war of power, there will be causalities. I'm just not willing to lose. If I do, then Diego will have it harder next year. Ninth grade will not go easily on him. He has to learn how to control himself now, or someone else will always do the controlling for him.

Principals always tell us, "Pick your battles," because they don't want to deal with hoodies and headphones.

Compliance is the lowest form of teaching. How can I expect this boy to read if I can't get him to follow two simple rules?

I go through the whole routine with his class. I rant a little at the biggest whiner, some good kid tells the whiner to apologize, I start teaching the *Deepest Fear* lesson to this class, and then I look right at Diego and say, "It is always about Man Versus Self, people. We will always have an internal struggle to choose right from wrong. Some of you chose wrong yesterday, some very wrong. I will have a sub again. The question is, what will you do then?"

There is power in choice. Because of my note, Diego will choose to take off his hoodie and headphones today. Tomorrow he'll do the same. Now I just have to get him to stop going to Pacheco to get his pobrecito fix.

"How'd today go?" Maggie asks. She knew all about the substitute's day, *a day from hell* is nothing in comparison to a day as a substitute teacher.

"It went all right," I say, but I don't mean it. I won't know how today went until the next time I take a day off.

"WIFM," Pacheco says. "We need to ask ourselves this when we're talking to our students about their benchmark scores."

"What's in it for me?" Maggie whispers.

We're in our professional development meeting, the one where we have bonding experiences like making paper helicopters and eating snacks for the first half hour and then get lectured about all things related to testing.

He told us to bring our computers.

"I believe you get to have seconds on the snack table," I whisper back. "Were you expecting something more exciting? I saw a Maserati today—is that what you were thinking?"

"I didn't think they made normal cars," she says.

"Oh, it was totally normal—probably a MUSD employee."

Pacheco pulls up the data he loves so much—the Promethean board is synonymous with data during PD.

"You can see from this chart, we are right in the middle of the other middle schools, but as you know, I'm competitive, and I really want—"

"To hit more balls," I whisper to Maggie.

"Exactly," she says.

Our reading scores have dipped below what he expected. "Our math scores are carrying us, people. We need to get our reading scores back up."

There's not a plan, just disappointment in our teaching and our follow-through of the district's awe-inspiring motto: Mission Unified Schools, the District Where Scores Soar!

"He should be a motivational speaker," I whisper to Maggie.

12

BOOKS OF WRATH

On the drive to work, it's Confession Friday, the entertainment industry's idea of a good time, callers confessing scandalous versions of philandering and deceit in weekly doses.

I envy those people.

How quaint it must be to have only your private-life transgressions radio-worthy, yet your job not so interesting, not so weighing on the psyche or tearing at the soul.

Even when I do it well, even when the strides gained are fifty feet long, there's always a constant reminder of what I've done wrong.

Perks of the job.

Freaking Emmy.

His full name is Emmanuel Mario Medina II, and he's a normal student in a normal class with normal grades from a (Mission Heights) normal home, and he just ruined my entire week.

Kids finish books in here all day long. Yesterday Emmy finished *All American Boys*. No biggie.

This is what we do, and this particular boy had been quizzed enough to assure me he's really reading.

"How'd you like it?" I said. "What'd you think?"

Most of the time the answer is about the plot or about a character and how he changes or a character and what she does differently than anyone in her family has ever done.

Apparently, Emmy didn't read the pat-answer playbook.

"You know how a tiny pebble thrown into water has a ripple effect? And you know the idea that the ripple here can cause a tsunami thousands of miles away? It was like that."

"What?" I said, but I didn't mean "what," I meant, "WTF?"

"You know how the ripple effect happens? This book is like that—there's this tiny event, but it leads to something so much bigger."

I just stared at him.

"That's what it made me think of," he said, continuing as if to clarify, as if my dumbfounded look was an indication of inadequately understanding his beautiful answer. He smiled sweetly at me, like I was the one with the problem.

Usually this stupid confession show is a relief from reality, yet today I think of calling in to the show. I want to explain my side of the story, how the state only cared about test scores, how the district panders to the state, how teachers pander to parents, and parents pander to their children. I want to call those ridiculous radio show hosts and let the entire city of Tucson know it's all Ed's fault. He's the one who prevented me from asking more of my students; he's the one who put the ceiling above my head.

The inane caller uses his one minute of fame to defame himself for the sake of scandal. Apparently, he drank too much last night and ended up naked on his roommate's floor and doesn't remember a thing. "I slipped out of the room before he woke up, though," he says.

"But where is your underwear?" the show's hosts want to know.

But do we?

Does anyone?

What about a teacher confession?

Would anyone want to know?

"You know most of them live in Barrio Sobaco?"

"What's that?" I say.

"The Armpit Barrio," he says.

Mark and I are standing in the hallway, looking for hooligans committing possible shenanigans. We test the air for wafts of reefer, we listen for whispered plans, we watch for suspicious camaraderies.

He knows nothing of my Emmy angst.

"Our kids live in the armpit barrio?"

Sobaco is not Barrio Anita, with the warmest tortillas, or Barrio Hollywood, with its Low Rider weekend, cars bouncing on hydraulics, Santana playing loud enough to rattle the windows. Our kids live in Barrio Sobaco, the one in need of a shave and deodorant.

"Freaking Jesus," I mumble as Abel and Little Boy Irony walk past us. "I've seriously never heard of it," I add. "Armpit is the worst name I've ever heard for a barrio."

"That's where Abel, Jesus, and Gero live—tons of my basketball kids live there," says Mark. He goes on to describe the neighborhood where the armpit lies and the streets surrounding it.

Rodriguez walks up and hears Sobaco and Mark's description. "That's Barrio Hoyo," she says. "Barrio Sobaco is further south. Don't you guys know your barrios?"

Mark asks Mrs. T.

She describes the area closer to A Mountain.

"Oh my God—why doesn't anybody actually know where this barrio is? I don't get it, why so complicated?"

"Why is what so complicated?" Maggie says as she swings open her door.

"Where Barrio Sobaco is," someone says.

"Sobaco? It's by Tully," says Maggie.

"No, it's by Maxwell," someone says.

"Next to the railroad tracks," someone else says.

A gaggle of teachers now, talking all at once, not one person agreeing with another, no one quite able to find Sobaco on the map.

"It's behind Menlo Park."

"That's Barrio Menlo."

"There's no such thing as Barrio Menlo."

"You guys are clueless," someone says. "It's right behind the mission on Sixth."

Suddenly six staff members sniff the air.

"Uh oh," says Mark. "Someone's being dumb in the boys' bathroom—I got this." He turns and walks away just as the bell rings.

We all want to linger, find out where the armpit is, but the passing period clock is always ticktocking, and teachers need to be near their rooms when class begins in order to restore order before it begins to crack.

Maggie pulls up her doorstop with her foot and begins to close her door, stopping to say, "Where are you from? Barrio Flowing Wells, right?"

"Yeah, right," I say.

"What's it like over there?" she says.

"Actually, like a week ago, one of my friends told me, back in the day, his mom said he couldn't ride his bike south of the Rillito River."

"He went to Amphi?"

"Yep."

"You're from across the river," she says.

I am from four walls and a roof over my head
Fifty yards away from rusted tin and broken glass
   Belching and beer guzzling
A certificate of higher education on the inside
A football field and broken chain link fence on the
outside
   Crotch scratching and innocence stealing just a
   football throw away

This is the poem example I don't write.

I would tell my students about the trailer park at the end of the cul-de-sac where I was raised. I'd describe the No Trespassing sign protecting the inhabitants of Lazy Saguaro Mobile Home Park from my family and our neighbors, but it's too late in the year now.

Not only that, but I'd sound silly not knowing exactly where their homes lie, Barrio Sobaco an unknown location, rolling the r's of "barrio" not a substitution for not knowing where my students live.

Do they really have to know I don't know?

Dammit.

Confession Friday isn't real; it's just a show, right?

Even now when I visit my parents, I want to call someone, tell them about the sign on the wrong side and about Jimmy Tanner.

We met three streets over on Greenlee. He was in seventh and I was in sixth. We played football, although, to be fair, smear-the-queer was the game of choice in 1977.

Jimmy and I were going steady just before the sun went down, and I heard a familiar whistle in the air.

"That's my dad," I said. "I gotta go, but I'll come back."

Jimmy was my first boyfriend, and I was quite committed to that ten-minute love affair, going back to Greenlee a day later to celebrate our first forty-eight hours.

"I want you to meet my parents," he said.

I'd never actually been to the Lazy Saguaro. Before Jimmy, I had never known anyone who actually lived there, the chain-link fence separating the park and my hood too long, the boarded windows and broken cars too ominous. I'm not a fence jumper, and, of course, there was the No Trespassing sign.

"That's for strangers," Jimmy said. "But you're my girl-friend—come on."

We squeezed between the broken pieces of chain link and walked hand and hand up to his parents on their picnic chairs parked on the slab in front of his trailer, a pile of beer cans growing.

When Jimmy said, "This is my father, James Sr.," I let go of Jimmy Jr.'s hand, emulating my father's handshakes, business at hand, nice to meet you, and all that adultlike stuff.

Mr. Tanner looked me up and down, a tasty prime rib in the butcher's glass. My hand still warm from Jimmy's, he looked at the fruit of his loins and asked, "Cork her yet?"

I am from teenage corkscrews and beer-can gardens

I don't know why I'm even saying this; this isn't even my real problem. My confession is not about my childhood, and it's certainly not about Ed and his pals.

Freaking Emmy.

My freshmen year, Flowing Wells High School, circa 1981, my words articulate, my diction acute, my excitement border-ing on contagious when I announce to my high school English class my late-night discovery. "I found a symbol in *The Grapes of Wrath*."

My teacher was not impressed. "That's not a symbol."

"But, but—" I said.

"The symbols are outlined in the handout on your desk," she said.

I wanted to ask if she'd partied with Steinbeck or if he'd left a study guide, maybe "The Secret Symbols of Grapes of Wrath Revealed" was in her Teaching English 101 class. I didn't know; maybe she knew. Only part of me knew she was wrong, but it wasn't the confident part of me.

"But there was this other thing with the—"

"The handout is on your desk," she said.

"Bradenton?" said one of my brothers, my junior year. My freshmen disappointment had not deterred me. I was eager and ready to learn. "She sucks," he said.

"She hates us," said another.

Sometime before the winter break, she assigned our class *The Old Man and the Sea*.

"It's so skinny," I whispered to the girl next to me.

"I heard it was gay," she whispered back.

I read it in one night.

The next day Mrs. B. acted as though I'd committed treason against Hemingway, a heinous form of high school English blasphemy right up there with dangling my participles.

"You were assigned to read up to page fifty."

I told her I couldn't help it.

"You were supposed to only read to fifty," she said again, hand on hip, snap of her gum grating on my last teenage nerve.

I told her I couldn't help it again. I loved that book—the struggle, the triumph, the feeling I had when I finished in my bedroom, no one's interpretation except my own—yet all my ignorance and all my limitations were too much for Bradenton to bear.

She wouldn't let it go and threatened to call my dad, the principal, the school board, security.

By my senior year of high school, my sexuality was not the only clandestine topic but so was my reading: John Irving, Marion Zimmer Bradley, Stephen King, all behind my Shakespeare-loving teacher's backs.

"That's trash," whispered in the hallways.

"Not real literature," lectured in Sunday service five days a week.

"But I can feel it," I told my best friend, Julie, my first crush, the only one who understood my dilemma.

"It doesn't matter what anyone says. Read what you want," she said, savvy to the ways of society, understanding the difference between actually reading and the reading we did when we were assigned books like criminals. Read this, do this, do that—a regiment of what to read, how to feel, how to react, how to memorize.

I'm stalling.

High school isn't my issue either, reminiscing over my experiences only exacerbates my naiveté, my illiteracies and inadequacies.

In junior college I struggled through text by Gloria Steinem and Kafka, Joyce and Homer. I was in pain, text forced upon me like a railroad worker on the chain gang, a rain of sweat underneath my orange jumpsuit.

And then I got Dr. Bauman in the College of Education at Florida State, where I heard we would learn how to teach reading.

"Read what we want?" we said.

"Read what you want," she said.

Surely this was more educational blasphemy. Who would read *Huckleberry Finn* if not by force?

I started with the best sellers like *Cider House Rules* by Irving and *Tales of the City* by Maupin. As I gained confidence, I moved toward the classics my English teachers hadn't forced upon us, like *Catcher in the Rye*, *The Great Gatsby*, and *The Sun Also Rises*.

By November my reading palette had grown exponentially. I was more confident in my choices, riskier in my selections. Then my roommate told me to read *Their Eyes Were Watching God* by Zora Neale Hurston.

"I don't even know what she's saying," I said.

The dialect was too Southern for my general American vocabulary and my Arizona genes. My lack of ability embarrassed me, but my roommate understood.

"Try *The Color Purple* first. That dialect can be hard too, but it's not as hard, then you can try *Their Eyes*."

She was a PhD candidate in biology, not an English major in buzzkill. I did as she suggested and made it from one book to another in the baby steps I needed.

"I don't even know which one I like better," I said.

"Yeah, me either," she said, our common language understood, no book report *necessito*, no Cliff Notes perused to tell us the author's purpose.

When the semester was over, I felt accomplished but confused. We were college students who could already read, already successful with two years of college behind us, a future so bright ahead, but I was going back to Tucson, Arizona, to Mission Unified School District. How could I possibly do this with nonreaders? And reader haters?

I couldn't.

So I didn't.

Instead I spent every morning pouring a little dash of hypocrisy into my coffee cup and setting off for work.

Twenty years of confessional Fridays cannot make up for my failures.

For all the parents out there who forgive themselves their own trespasses, a shout-out: way to overcome the guilt of parenting, the humiliation of not winning the elusive Parent of the Year...

Dammit.

This isn't easy.

I've done so much wrong.

Dear Luis, I'm sorry I wasn't a better listener.

Annais, I'm sorry I didn't push you more.

Alany, sorry I didn't help with those bruises.

Sorry I yelled at you in the hallway.

In the class.

Didn't hear.

Didn't see.

Didn't know.

Didn't.

Did.

I feel nauseous and nauseated.

Refusing to succumb to the voices in my head, I carried on, forged forward. I was a dynamic teacher with alternative assessments instead of book reports, clever "book extensions" instead of poster-board displays.

I had plays and video presentations, books-in-a-box, and rap song remixes.

I made the books I assigned interesting, I provided depth and understanding, I had successful kids reading book upon book upon book.

I did.

I swear.

I think I'm going to be sick.

Dear Students 1989–2008,

I am sorry for every book I told you to read, every book report I ever made you write, every diorama and book project, for believing you when you said you read when we both know I didn't even read the books I was assigned (except *The Old Man and the Sea*, and we both know how that went). I'd love to say I was naïve, when in fact I was negligent.

Sincerely,
Ms. Russell

I was teaching English-language learners, and everyone had their own book. I would ask my pat questions, they'd give their pat answers, and we were happy. People were "reading."

Then one day I asked a question I couldn't answer.

The student had a book I'd never read and knew nothing about. "I'm done," she said.

I had no reason to doubt her. I wasn't even trying to trick her.

I opened up a random chapter and read the first sentence. "What happens here?" I asked.

The girl hemmed and hawed. I picked another page, asked another question.

More hemming and hawing...

I told everyone to stop what they were doing.

I walked around from student to student asking questions that could have been answered if the reading was real, but no one could answer any direct, exact question I asked.

I was still a failure.

My kids couldn't read, and I was their accomplice. I was no better than the class-set reading teacher spoon-feeding depth, cutting up little pieces of understanding into bite-sized, edible chunks for chewing by anyone.

By everyone.

Freaking Confession Friday.

Eff you.

What do you know anyway?

I took a class once, thirty teachers in a circle espousing their personal teacher stories, how they landed back into a classroom for most of their adult lives.

Twenty-eight people started somewhere else—engineers, housewives, insurance salesmen—a variety of jobs, a variety of paths leading to the same destination. Only two of us chose teaching first, our destinies written out, stepping stones leading only one direction. In our circle this spunky newer teacher confessed to teaching her stuffed animals to read and write and complete simple math calculations.

"I never considered something else," I said. "My dad was a teacher."

I remember that day, a superior feeling. I was better than all those other teachers, late bloomers all of them, except the stuffed teddy bear teacher, she and I were equals.

I didn't know there was anything else. I was so naïve, so isolated from the extraordinary I became the ordinary, what I saw, what I knew firsthand. It wasn't an actual choice among choices. It was the only choice among one choice.

A. Teacher

I can't even say I failed to become an astronaut or psychologist or air force pilot.

I didn't even try.

Confirmation bias is a dangerous sedative.

Dear Faculty and Staff,

I had one job, and I still couldn't do it.

Regrets,
Ms. R.

No need to put my full name; everyone doesn't need to know it's me.

In 2009 I had a friend who was going to school in the UK. While she was gone, she wrote me an email: Read *The Book Thief.*

We'd talked books before, shared books in the past—our relationship wasn't built on books, but books were part of the base, mortar for the cracks.

I bought it.

I opened it.

I read the first chapter and thought about texting her. This guy's language was not mine, his concept not one I was interested in reading. I had to tell her I couldn't do it. I wanted to say, "This reminds me of the time you recommended that one book you hadn't read in its entirety and then told me to read it, only to find out the ending sucked—I'm still mad at you," but I didn't.

I let *The Book Thief* sit on the coffee table.

It stayed there until one day I saw my partner reading it.

She said someone else told her to read it. "You just have to get past that beginning," she said, and then she explained the narrator, what she liked, why I should give it another try.

A second and third opinion, maybe I was missing something on that first go-around. I planned to try again after she finished, the ending being so important.

A month later, tears streaming down her face, barely getting out the words, she said, "You have to read this."

Crying?

I wasn't sure I wanted to cry. I do cry, I have cried, but my job is sad enough. I don't need extra tears.

I made a second attempt anyway. There had to be something in there I didn't see, some treasure chest I was sure to find, more gold doubloons in my life, but this time mine, all mine, no Bradenton to tell me about the themes and symbols.

Before I even opened *The Book Thief*, I had to prepare myself, that first attempt not far from my psyche, the apprehension of the commitment I was making to this relationship quite significant. I can only read one book at a time—should this be that book?

I entered the pages as one might enter a winter-morning swim, a difficult time moving, my eyes not quite in sync with the rest of me.

But then, days later, it was quite obvious why my friends loved this book, the protagonist worthy of our support, a boy worthy of our admiration, a papa full of love and a mama seething with complication, the narrator forgiving and kind, kind enough to expose the future long before we get there, the reader the last one to understand that people will die. It's WWII; of course people die.

I texted my friend, "Am I going to hate you when I finish this?"

She replied, "I don't know. Maybe. Probably."

I forged on, expecting the normal crying associated with death, the sadness that permeates reality with words in my head, people I've never met breaking my heart.

I would like to report I was prepared. I had spent a lifetime reading, not reading like the voracious, but enough like the sufficient.

And I've cried, of course.

A teaching tradition, I cried yearly reading *Stone Fox* out loud to my second graders.

Sobbing when I read *Where the Red Fern Grows* to my fifth graders.

Bawling over *Bridge to Terabithia* to my sixth graders.

I cried when I read *The Education of Little Tree*, the thought of the love portrayed from grandfather to grandson everything I wish for my students.

The Power of One, when I realized Courtenay was speaking to me, letting me know it's okay to be the best I could be.

Just sayin', I'm a crier, love lost, love found, dog died, dog lived—doesn't matter. I embrace, I feel, I choke up years later just thinking about what I've read.

The narrator couldn't scare me out of continuing. I was ready to cry, prepped, peppered, and prepared. Bring it, Death; you can't take me anywhere I've never been.

Yet, he did.

The narrator waved his death wand haphazardly, an atomic bomb of his own, killing everyone except three. One was out of town during the barrage of explosions, and another was likely in her own bomb shelter, shielded by power and money.

The third was the protagonist, alone in the basement, writing her own book, the pages scrawled out in purposeful child prose, the walls protecting her from the fury outside.

My mind raced backward to the number of times the author repeated himself.

How many times did he have to say it before I understood?

I'd been remiss, teaching reading completely wrong, repeating the same punishment my teachers inflicted upon me, assuring myself I wasn't like them; I made reading out loud fun instead of dreary and dreadful, gave Esteban confidence, helped so many kids on the reservation, so many other students on my list of things I'd done right.

I wasn't a terrible teacher.

I did something with Sabrina, I was sure of it.

I was angry with the author, his narrator lulling me in to believing death was the saddest thing I'd experience. Maybe he thought I'd miss the book thief's parents or her boyfriend or all the people in the village, but I didn't. Sure, that was sad, but that wasn't what killed me.

In his book, the carnage of death, spending countless hours to write five hundred pages to say one thing, making a mockery of my years of teaching reading with read-alouds and whole-class sets and book reports and dioramas, Zusak made me see my teaching as not only obsolete but also as a socially acceptable form of educational malpractice.

I knew reading was important.

I knew reading was the way out of the Barrio Sobacos of the world, but until I read it, until I felt it, I didn't really understand that books save lives.

I bawled for a half hour. I cried harder than I'd ever cried before. I mourned my inadequacies as a teacher, all my short-comings, all my downfalls, so many fake readers I trusted, so many book reports graded on fake reading.

I mourned what I could have done for children but didn't do, so many students I had wronged.

I texted my friend. "I hate you."

A half hour later, after I'd wiped away the tears and began my amends to the hundreds of students in my past, I wrote back. "What made you cry?"

She wrote back. "I didn't."

No one I know read *The Book Thief* the same way I did—no teacher, no friend.

I'd be a hypocrite to espouse the intent of a man I've never met, but it doesn't matter, does it? I was wrong, and I had to change.

In 2010 I started not believing anyone was reading and aligned my day into two rules: read all the words; make connections to those words.

And until yesterday I was feeling pretty successful.

Freaking Emmy.

If he'd just told me the plot or something special about a character, then maybe I could have skipped right through this final phase of teaching unscathed.

Abel isn't the only one with forty-five days left of school.

Not a confession.

Deb Sinclair was my surrogate mother since I was eleven, my softball coach since I was fourteen, my sexual-orientation guide since I saw my first known lesbian.

She handed me *To Kill a Mockingbird*, and somewhere around this time we watched the movie.

In the scene where Mr. Robinson must stand and accentuate the uselessness of his left hand, I stared at his arm. I kept watching for trickery, whether it was a cinematic oversight or an acting flaw, but I obsessed.

"He moved his arm," I said.

I don't remember if she guffawed, but she should have. I was so juvenile. In that moment I knew the book's emphasis on the racism of the South was there. It's so obvious, but I already knew that. What wasn't obvious was my own racism.

Between the book and the movie, I forced myself to reflect. Sinclair didn't make me reflect; that was on my own.

Other than two conversations with Sinclair from that evolutionary time period, it's more of the essence of Sinclair that has permeated my skin. That book, the story, she gave me the gift of reflection.

That's what teachers do.

Freaking Emmy.

That's what students do.

To Every Student I've Ever Had,

I am sorry.

Love,
Ms. Russell

How many children did I spoon-feed before I realized they're ready to chew on their own?
How many did I think were reading and weren't?
And couldn't?
Now Emmy makes me realize my years of questions have been too leading, my methods too simplistic.
Yet, I'd be remiss to say I have any idea what he went through, what he understood, what stayed with him, what haunts him now.
I realize now my questions have always been about plot and character and were restrictive in their insight as well as their polarizing account of what the reader went through. Who am I to narrow down their answer into something more digestible to me?
My students not only didn't read, but so many of them couldn't read, and now that the climate has changed, I have not been keeping up with the times. My sales team, people like Manny who get people like Abel to read, is in full force now. The changes are occurring. I just need to keep up.
It really is Confession Friday.
I would call, but no one would understand a teacher's lament.

13

OBJECTS OF RETENTION

I had a friend once who got a late-night call over the summer from a student. He was crying so hard, it took my friend a minute to understand. "Why aren't you coming back?" the boy said, through his sniffling and sobs.

"What do you mean? I'll be there just like normal," said my friend.

The boy said his mother had gone to the school board meeting where they voted to discontinue the shop teacher's class.

"That couldn't have happened," he said, "no one told me a thing."

This is my first thought when my pop calls to tell me there's an article in Sunday's paper about my district. I'm almost sure MUSD hasn't discontinued my job, but I'm also thinking of having some friends over and starting a new drinking game. We'll each take turns telling stories, and whenever someone can relate to the story being told, then we'll have to do a shot.

After just a few rounds, all my friends will need a cab.

I'm going to call it MUSD PTSD.

"I guess the courts just figured out how to improve racial diversity," my dad said, my sugary Sunday morning coffee still warm in my hand, my entire life's work in question on this nonwork day. "MUSD wants to match the race of the students with the teachers in the school," he adds.

Of course they do.

"First they'll try to get us to volunteer to change schools and when that doesn't work, they'll offer us bonus money, and if that doesn't work, they'll force us to switch," I say.

"Sounds about right," he says.

We talk for a bit more before we hang up. He always needs to leave me with a story of some student's success, something to keep me focused on the important part of my job.

"Have a good week," he says.

Funny he should say that.

According to Pacheco's weekly bulletin, there is nothing planned the entire week. There is no holiday, no fire drill, no testing, no assemblies, pep or otherwise, no orchestra concerts, no science fairs, no guest speakers, picture day is long gone, the weather forecast is eighty to ninety degrees with no rain or snow or sleet or hail in our immediate future.

Plus, the library is open.

"Thanks, Pop. I will," I say, but I don't mean it. There's nothing more ominous to a teacher than blue skies.

Twenty-four hours later, I wish I'd taken the day off work.

"I've read the article they're referencing," I say, the Sunday morning coffee gone from my hand, to Ms. Rodriguez, the first person I see at school Monday morning.

"Fucking special master," she says.

"You know," I say, "I'll never get used to that name. How is it that the guy who is here to correct us of our racism has the most racist job title in history?"

"Grand dragon was already taken," she says.

"You know what he wants, right? It's unconscionable," I say.

"Did you hear the superintendent's justification? He said the first Hispanic teacher he ever had was when he was in college— told him he should drop out of mechanical engineering and go into English."

"I stand corrected," I say. "That's unconscionable."

We're walking through the corridors of our campus, children buzzing to and fro, no idea how angry many of the adults are now or will be by the end of the day.

I spend the first part of my morning telling everyone I see, "You know the Unitary Status Plan is because of a court case?"

MUSD versus Thompson and Bernal has been on the books since 1975.

For my fellow colleagues who were born after 1975, I let them know we were still in the Vietnam War and it's the same year Betamax was invented.

"Betawhat?" the young teachers say.

"There's a court case?" the veteran teachers say.

"Do you know the plaintiffs don't agree?" I say too, because I want everyone to be informed that one family believes in neighborhood schools and doesn't want their children bused across town and the other family doesn't believe in neighborhood schools and wants their children bused across town.

And the research referenced in the newspaper?

It stresses the importance of teacher recruitment from underrepresented groups.

"The research doesn't say racially profile all your teachers and move them around according to a box marked on their application packet," says someone.

"Do they care that we applied to schools where we actually want to work?" says someone else.

All morning there's a fervor in the hallways and the breeze-ways, the courtyard and the classrooms, partially my fault but mostly MUSD's, all the excitement Pacheco's calendar could not possibly predict.

Luckily the special master from Baltimore has been hired to fix our district...just in time for me to apply for that exterminating job.

I bring this up because there is an upturned cockroach at my door. As I step over the recently deceased, I think about Ed and the fact that I'm positive he never mentioned the potential for cockroach infestation at my future worksite.

I've seriously become a cockroach expert.

I say this with complete humility. I'm thinking an additional retirement income in pest removal would definitely be within my skill set. When they ask about my experience with cockroaches, I can honestly say I worked with them every day for almost thirty years.

After school last Friday, we all had to empty our classroom cabinets so the custodians could hose down the little hosers without worrying about a teacher's yard sale scores cluttering up the spraying space. Pipe cleaners and tongue depressors, old *National Geographic* magazines, and cardboard egg cartons hiding little brown balls with so much baby-making potential.

"Gotta get all those egg sacks—if you know what I mean," said the p.m. custodian as I left for the weekend. "It's those little suckers that keep on hatching—gotta get all those little critters." He laughed as he spoke, chuckling about his weekend killing spree.

We had no choice. The health inspector dropped by. Apparently, she was horrified by what she found, little black roach poopies in the corners, all those little brown egg sacks hidden in the dark.

I find a few more dead carcasses and toss them out before

checking my email and swinging open my door for the beginning of another melee Monday.

"Remember Debbie?" I ask Maggie as we stand at our stations.

"Which Debbie?" she says.

My early-morning emails made me nostalgic for those colleagues of long ago.

"The one who thought she was making connections with kids by lecturing them on how she has self-discipline and how they should have discipline." I put air quotes around the words "connections" and "self-discipline" because I'm feeling particularly funny.

"You mean the one who talked about discipline and got caught for cheating on her time sheets or the one who talked about discipline and called her kids *mija* and *mijo* all year because she couldn't be bothered to learn their names?"

I laugh. "I forgot about that second one—I want to call them The Incompetents." More air quotes. "You like?"

"It's catchy," she says.

The Incompetents are at the forefront of my mind as the retention lists and comments about the students on those lists fill my morning email inbox. I don't attend the grade-level meetings, so I'm not privy to the names until they are almost finalized, but when I see one particular name on the eighth-grade list, my reaction is immediate.

Despite pressing *reply to all*, my email is meant for Weiss. There's no doubt she's the headhunter of this particular expedition. "I cannot meet during your team planning, so email is the only way I can communicate with all of you. Can someone provide some evidence as to why Manny is a good candidate for retention? What was his Light's Scale score? Or/and can we have a team vote?"

I wait for an answer, but I can guess Weiss's reasons. "Manny has a bad attitude and refuses to work, he's constantly disruptive, and I have to send him out all the time—he does nothing for me." But she doesn't write that; she doesn't write anything.

We're colleagues, Weiss and I, not friends.

My friends and I have one important commonality.

"Kids are number one and number two and number three— if I come up with a number four, I'll let you know."

My dad's words.

His license plate still says KDSRNO1.

I understand what these teachers want.

They are carnivores.

They crave meat.

The Light's Retention Scale consists of nineteen questions regarding a child's size, maturation, transience, etc. All factors considered, the reasoning behind the scale is to accurately predict the potential success of a child who is retained versus the success of that same student not retained. The final score is used as a determinant to hold the child back or move them along.

A student with a barely younger sibling is a poor candidate.

A student who attends school every day is a good one.

A child with emotional issues is a poor one.

I'm in the middle of mentally adding Manny's number when a friend from the eighth-grade team walks into my room.

"They need you next door," she says. "They're talking about Manny."

I don't know what to expect as I walk out into the hallway and one door down into a room of twelve or so teachers. The math teacher is talking as I slip into the room and lean against the counter near the door.

It appears the entire eighth-grade team is present, which includes the teacher in the corner moving his thumbs in rapid fire on his phone. When he tips the screen just enough, I can see the bright candy colors of a video game.

Other people have actual Xanax. I have fantasy headlines.

Teacher Brawl at Mission Heights Middle School Leaves Teachers in a Tizzy

The science teacher says, "Manny hasn't even put his name on a paper."

The language arts teacher says he struggles with completing projects. "He has a thirty-nine percent," she says. "And that's a modified grade based on his attendance."

I'm still staring at the teacher playing the video game when he stops his fingers, looks up, and says, "My turn?" He looks around the room for confirmation. When no one says anything, he says, "Manny doesn't pay attention to the instructions, so he's constantly off task."

Someone says, "He never tries."

"He's a distraction."

"He's rude."

The math teacher, literally my source of hope for the future of teaching, finally speaks. "I do have to agree with my colleagues about Manny's behavior, but I also need to say that he has made progress—just the other day he earned a C on a math test—just when I thought he wasn't paying attention, he goes and does well on something that was fairly difficult, even for my better students."

She says more about his successes than his failures, and when there are failures, they are her own. "If I could just get him to come in a couple times at lunch, then I think he could squeeze by with a D, but it hasn't happened yet."

It's difficult to navigate these waters. This isn't my team; many of us are just colleagues and not necessarily congenial ones. "I don't believe retention will help Manny, although I do believe consistent expectations will help—"

A teacher who doesn't have Manny interrupts me midsentence and addresses the room. "Do you even belong here?" he says, not even bothering to look at me. "I'm serious. Why are you even here? We've been talking about this boy for months, and you haven't said a word."

I oscillate between the candy crusher and the back of this teacher's head.

Hey, guys, Ed called. He wants his diplomas back.

A few years ago, a colleague came into my room, looked around at all my little readers, looked back at me, and asked me what I'd done to them. "I know these guys—I've never seen them like this."

I took a minute and explained my philosophy and my technique. "I had a student once who read thirty-five books in one year, and like most of my students, she came into class having never read a single book."

These were his students too, my class the supplemental version to his language arts class.

"How do you know she wasn't lying?" he said.

"I ask them questions individually, and they have to answer correctly or they won't get points for the book."

My colleague looked around the room one last time, looked me up and down, and said, "I can't do that—I'm worried about accountability."

Me too, I wanted to say.

I wanted to explain that the heft of a book can no more be measured by a book report than a student's growth can be measured by seventy-five bubbles, but I don't believe he wanted to hear my thoughts, this particular teacher's idea of teaching based solely on demand and supply, something easily translated into an alphabet letter and documented into a grade book.

I'm certain Manny has read more books since he started our school than any of his executioners, but that won't help him now.

Accountability.

Where is she when you need her?

Before I can answer whether or not I belong in this decision of Manny's future, Weiss intervenes. "Let's table this discussion for another time. I think we all have a great deal to think about—don't you?"

No one disagrees.

I head back to class.

It's all I can do to refocus.

I want to rant and rave to my friend as I take my class back over, but she needs to get somewhere, and curse words aren't for kids.

"Later," I say.

"Definitely," she says. "Oh, and one more thing, I guess Gero finished his book."

I turn to my little boy wonder. "You're lying," I say.

"Ah, Ms., why you so mean? Can I talk to you?"

He doesn't know, but I need Gero.

Like we have a drug deal going down, he whispers, "I finished that book you gave me, but"—he leans closer—"I told my brother to read it, so I don't have it with me." He leans back and grins. "Ms.," he says, drawn out, slowly, "that book was gooooood. That was way better than all the books you gave me."

I'm staring at him in disbelief, and then he says, "That part about his sister was sad, wasn't it?"

Freaking Gero!

"What, Ms.? You don't believe me, do you? I can prove it. Ask me anything. I know everything about it."

I have never met this kid. If he were in a police lineup and someone asked which one was Gero, I wouldn't pick him.

He leans in closer and whispers almost inaudibly. "Ms., do you have *Perfect Chemistry*?"

Unbelievable.

I laugh, of course. Gero begging for books is about as beautiful as my job gets.

"Answer the questions first, and then we'll talk about *Perfect Chemistry*—why do you want to read it anyway?"

It's hard not to laugh in times like these. It's all funny, his innocence, his purpose, his intent.

"Abel says it changed his perspective on girls," he says. "Ms., don't laugh. I want to know about girls."

Gero may not know about girls, but he knows me enough to realize he'd never get *Perfect Chemistry* if he hadn't finished *True Diary*, my love for Alexie too deep to be ignored.

I ask Gero what happened to the protagonist's sister, ask him what the English teacher said about Arnold, and what the teacher said about the sister.

He knows the simplistic answers to prove he read, but that's not what I want to know.

It's hard being a reading teacher. I have this overwhelming desire to chew up the theme and feed all the baby birds in the forest.

"What's the point of the book?" I say. "Why in the world would I want you to read it?"

"To know we can overcome stuff," he says.

He's not sure, of course. This is his first book. What has happened to him since that first page is much more than can be answered with even the best of questions, but "overcome stuff," yes—long after he forgets what happened in *True Diary*—he will never forget the fact that he can overcome.

I look at the calendar on my desk, calculate the number of days we have left, throw in all the down time students have after testing while they wait for everyone to finish testing, couple all this with the drive of learning about girls, and suddenly I'm hopeful the little boy who refused to read will finish two books this year.

"Okay, Gero, I'm giving you *Perfect Chemistry*, but you better get started."

When I hand him the book, I can see five-year-old Gero next to the Christmas tree, the present he'd waited for all year now in his hands, only sparkly wrapping paper separating him from his future of fun.

"I got you, Ms.," he says, wide-eyed, walking away, already reading the first page, tripping over limbs attached to bodies and legs attached to chairs on the way back to his cornrow seat.

I look up at the clock.

Why isn't it moving?

I decide to scrap my lesson plan with Abel's class. I'm in no mood to teach a lesson meant to challenge the status textbook quo. I just tell these people to do other people's work, the homework they've been avoiding, the assignment shoved into the bottom of their bag.

Or read.

"You can keep reading if you want," I say.

At least ten don't even look up, like I never said anything anyway.

I'd like to report that I do some centering breathing, that I mediate just a little or pray to the saint of middle school teachers, but I don't, preferring instead to perseverate over the weatherman's forecast, the 75 percent chance I'd be punchy today with a chance of sarcasm. My students don't bother with weather reports anyway. They wear sweatshirts in the summer, teeny-tiny shorts in the winter. They travel as hurricanes, rendering useless my umbrella.

Third period is all this and more.

Everyone in my next class period needs something—three to the bathroom, five without pencils, one to the nurse, one to the counselor, three to see different teachers about grades, and two don't have their books today.

"I was reading last night, and I left it on my dresser," says one.

"My sister took my book and hid it," says the other.

The phone rings, it's the school nurse, and she wants to see a student.

Five minutes go by, and all I can do is get paper passed out, another five to get the attention of any remaining students, and we've already read for twenty minutes, so I have a solid twenty-five minutes of teaching, if all goes well.

Loewen told me what to teach but not how to teach it.

"We're going to look at this on the Promethean board—this is a chapter from a California textbook about the South—what do you all know about the South, about slavery, about the Civil War?"

I'm wound up. The giant electronic white board projects the subliminal racism of our American history textbook, and it agitates me.

"Who knows how the South made money?"

The answers are solid. Their eighth-grade social studies teachers would be proud they let these people out into the world.

"Growing cotton and tobacco," they say.

"And how did they ensure their workers worked?" I say.

"The slave owners used overseers to inflict punishment," they say.

"Slaves didn't get paid."

"Slaves were often branded."

Picking cotton was back breaking.

Painful.

Awful.

Deadly.

"Great," I say, "let's look at how the textbook describes what you all just said from your own experience, and then we'll compare."

The class is engaged. I feel the anger in my body begin to dissipate. I remind myself it's about the kids, just the kids. That's all that matters.

Words like "branded" and "back breaking" are never used, though, and when the author does use words, they're sweet candy coatings, simple to chew and easy to swallow.

"You can see right here." I point to the Promethean projection. "The author states, 'one out of fifty African Americans were free.'" I turn back to my class. "What does that mean?"

I expect some guesses, some, "African Americans were mostly free," and other misunderstandings, but all I hear is, "You're weird."

I stop. I know her voice. I know all my kids' voices.

"What did you just say?"

It's Maria, one of my favorites. "I didn't say anything," she says.

"Oh, yes you did," I say.

"I heard her too, Ms.," says another kid. "You said Ms. is weird."

"I did not," says Maria.

I ask her why she'd say that to me, but she won't answer. She continues to say she said nothing when we all heard something, the same thing—I'm weird. Weird why? Weird for what? Weird how?

What did I do that was weird?

Care?

Obsess?

Want to teach something complicated?

I can't speak another word. I turn my back to the class and stare at the Promethean board.

This is why teachers give worksheets.

It's so much easier than teaching.

What do I do?

Why did she say that?

How do I not cry?

Crying is not an option.

I look at the clock.

Five minutes, seven really, but I could quit teaching in five, and it won't be long enough for them to do anything except pass their papers into the basket.

Can I stand with my back to the entire class for five minutes?

I hear students telling her to say she's sorry.

Ten kids saying, "Say you're sorry."

She says nothing.

Our entire relationship hanging on a mumbled, "You're weird."

I stay facing the white board—it's easier this way, better than facing them. "According to this textbook, one out of fifty African Americans were free," I say, but I can hear it in my voice. I don't care anymore. "One out of fifty. Let's do the math. What are they not saying? What's the math they hope you cannot do?"

Silence.

No one knows what to say, what I'm saying, or how to get Maria to apologize, and now it's too late.

One "weird" later I don't care that our textbooks are written to blind, to enable, to render us ignorant and now speechless.

My door opens, and Abel walks into the dark, the glow of the projector the only illumination in the room.

This is not his class.

"Ms.?" he says. "I finished it."

I don't know even know what "it" is. Abel's reading something elusive, forward moving, a sprint for which I have no legs. And anyway, doesn't he know I am still trying to teach this lesson? My stumbling lecture still in midstride? Is he even aware the words of our nation's history are stamped across our bodies? Our conversation ten feet from the projector now casts our shadows onto the screen.

"Yes?" I say as he hands me *Hip-Hop High School* by Alan Sitomer, a book I haven't read, have no plans to read, and don't remember giving him.

"That book was lit," he says. "I am determining myself to go to college and get a scholarship," he continues, no idea his grammar is askew. The escalating chatter of class off task, no one caring about my textbook obsession, no one listening to me or to Abel.

He points to the last sentence. "See that?" he says over the din.

I look down at the last four words on the page glowing in the light of Southern slavery.

"See?" he says. "See that?" he says again. "I have a future."

Normally I'd blame Ed for this moment, but the real culprit seems to be seeping himself into my district. Later I'll ask Mark when I'm not crying, maybe with a shot of tequila in my hand, "Where's the special master when I really need him?"

Before I leave for the day, I check my email for round two of the Teachers versus Manny, but my inbox is empty. This doesn't stop me from obsessing over my colleagues' reasoning, the ex-lineman believing size matters and a smaller eighth grader is a better candidate than a larger one. I agree, though, size does matter, and I am pretty sure I could take him in a cage fight. He'd get winded quickly, and I'd go in for some hella tricky WWF move I'd learned in the '80s, growing up in a house full of boys. The alternative, of course, is to consider I'm wrong about retention, but then I think of Galileo. He too probably had some serious doubts about that sun-and-moon theory of his.

In a school setting, there is almost always a general consensus about how long a day was or a week was or a month or a year.

"I thought the month would never end," said on March 27, 28, 29, 30, and 31.

"I thought it was Friday," said on Thursday.

"Oh my God, for a minute I thought it was Monday," said on Friday.

Agreed.

Friday only came because God heard the whimper of middle school teachers, a five-day week much longer than the allotted five days everyone else on the planet received because of the nine hundred teeny, tiny young adults beginning to subconsciously sense the inklings of spring, teenage tulips beginning to teeter just in time for testing.

And I'm getting a new girl.

Perfect. One more test score to be slid silently into my personal achievement scorecard, averaged in as if there's an average score for four days of attendance.

I walk over to Maggie's to ask if she's getting her too, but when I get there, it's apparent the One-Up Club almost met without me.

"I'd be happy to tell the special master where to—"

"If Pacheco says one more time that—"

"Freaking Jesus better—"

My friends, they are in an uproar, and then I ask if anyone has the new girl.

"From the group home?" someone says.

The room goes silent.

Then the din starts up again.

"The last girl from that group home propositioned all our boys."

"And stole the pen caps to use as pipes."

"And took Rodriguez's phone—oh, geez, is Rodriguez getting this girl?"

I keep up with my lesson during the week. The thought of giving out Care Bear coloring worksheets as party prizes is strong, but the desire to teach the mathematics of the American Dream textbook is stronger.

Yesterday I said, "The book says, 'forty-nine out of fifty African Americans were slaves,' which means 250,000 African Americas were free, so if we just multiply forty-nine times 250,000, we get 12,250,000."

Manny said, "That's messed up."

This was the fourth day of the Longest Week of the Year (a title bequeathed multiple times per year), the class was in full-focus, and Manny was in his seat in full uniform. It felt so much like a holiday, I expected Santa to come bursting through the door at any minute with little baby God in his arms.

"What's messed up?" I said.

"They can make anything sound good, can't they?"

I wanted to say the authors aren't liars, just magicians, the kind who can get you to focus on what they want, but those are fancy teacher words for me to make myself happy, and Manny had already said what needed to be said. Four days of teacher torture worth one second of understanding.

"Yes, that's exactly the point," I said, and then I repeated his words for those in the back.

"The eighth-grade social studies team does a good job

providing you alternative sources for the information they deliver," I continue, "but it won't always be that way, and the internet is a perfect example of offering you misleading information."

Spring has its perks, children understanding concepts so elusive just months ago. By Friday I'm still contemplating suicide but only cutting one arm.

From my desk I can see Gero one hundred pages into his modern-day *Romeo and Juliet*, his eyes like a compass due north, not giving him *True Diary* earlier just another check on my chalkboard of mistakes.

I wave Abel over to see what's happened since he interrupted my class with his *Hip-Hop High*.

I ask if he's still on the retention list, but he doesn't know. Our school policy is not so forthcoming on decisions of this magnitude. I pull up his grades on the computer while he sits in front of me, the fresh scent of Old Spice wafting from his more-man-than-boy body.

"You still have an F in social studies and science, but it looks like you have a solid D, almost a C in math—you've been going in for help?"

"Yeah," he says. "During lunch for test corrections."

I swing my chair, cross one leg over the other, cross my arms too, and look straight at Abel. I never noticed how long his legs are. I realize he looks almost uncomfortable sitting on the stool, towering above me.

Towering above me.

I almost didn't notice.

Abel isn't slouched over in his weary puppy pose.

"Dude," I say, "you have to pick between social studies and science—which one can you make into a D?"

"Oh, Ms.," he says, "There is no way I can catch up in social studies."

I look back at the computer, twenty empty spaces stare back me.

"Okay then you need to talk to the science teacher—ask him exactly what you need to do. Tell him there aren't any cute girls in seventh grade. He'll understand."

"I can do that," he says.

"You have to do that," I say. "Friday we put in progress grades—and yours are going to suck—and then you have exactly five weeks, even less because we input grades before the last day."

I try to sound tough, but I don't feel tough, and I'm smiling of course. The "no cute girls in seventh grade" is pretty funny stuff.

And it's not an exaggeration to say I'm terrified. Abel's science teacher may not let go of all those zeros. Teachers, sometimes like pit bulls, hold students in their craw and shake violently, but I can't say that about the science teacher. He's a reasonable man and a dedicated teacher.

"What are you reading?" I say.

"I just finished *Hip-Hop High School*—remember? But you didn't give me anything, and I've been working on my other classes, but now I'm ready."

"What do you want?"

"I want *Homeboyz* because it's the one after *Hip-Hop*, but Manny said you gave him *Always Running*, and he liked it, so I want that too."

"Both?"

"Yeah, is that okay?"

Abel is about to outread his family, his girlfriend, his future girlfriends, all of his current friends, and his future boss.

"Sure, that's okay," I say. "They are different enough that you should be able to keep them straight, and it will be good for your brain."

I'm lying, of course, not in my words but in my hopeful

tone. I am always leery and weary, perpetually cursed by the inability to trust any of my kids are going to turn out okay much less read two books at the same time.

It would be good for his brain, though. I've just never had a student actually read two at a time, and his grades are still questionable enough that he may be dragged into the retention vortex and I'll have to fight with everyone about Abel too, and I'm not even done fighting about Manny.

I check my email before leaving for the day.

Weiss says we should talk again next week, but she adds that Manny's behavior "deteriorated" this week. "He just did a nose dive over the last five days," she says. "I am even more adamant that another year of middle school will help better prepare him for high school."

I suppose professional development time would be the best place to discuss how the most marginal children are the ones retained. Maybe we could chitchat about the fact that retention is an outdated policy that potentially should never have been a policy.

Weiss's email makes me want to write a letter up the governmental food chain.

Dear United States Secretary of Education:

It's okay to change policies based on fallacies. Someone once thought thalidomide was a good idea too.

Yours Truly,
Daphne Russell

Maybe I should cc the special master. He might be interested to know he could use his influence to stop a real injustice, the universal end of retention not as racist as his current manhunt.

14

BOOK PUSHING

"Do you know what he looks like?"

"I heard he was like eighty and walked with a cane—introduced himself as the special master, and some old-school administrator told him it was 2017 and he wasn't about to call him 'master.'"

It's hard to know what brought us here—the excitement of next week's testing schedule, the gooey feeling Mark and I get when we think of administrators of long ago with their long-sleeved shirts and saucer-sized cojones . . . or the two-for-one teacher prices when we order off the Recess! drink list.

Regardless, this district loves us even if our other one doesn't.

"I was only asking because I keep picturing him as a member of the KKK."

Although it's doubtful he'll walk into this bar with the hood and robe, it's pretty safe to say the special master and the KKK both believe in what they're doing.

"Did you hear the next part of the plan?" Mark continues. "The public is demanding that our test scores should match our teacher evaluations."

"So, I'm a D if my students are Ds?"

Seriously.

If schools score too high, the state makes the test harder. Too low, they make the test easier. Test preparers make a science out of synchronizing test scores into the perfect bell curve. Apparently, I'm still in a letter-writing mood.

To Whom It May Concern,

The bell curve is manufactured pseudoscience turned into educational policy meant for astronomy, not social science. Despite your best efforts, a child's experiences cannot be mathematically regulated.

Sincerely,
Your Faithful Public Servant

I haven't yet retired, so I'll have to sign this one anonymously. No need to lose my state retirement over a little misunderstanding of an archaic, ill-formed concept like the curve.

Despite the end of the week coming toward me like a slow-motion mudslide, I had no time to process what was happening while it happened. Now, in this darkened version of a public school with graffiti, liquor, and loud noise, I don't think it's the best place to process my end of the week angst, yet, as the end of my career is careening, I have to take a moment to honor the endless moments of inspiration that happen on the daily.

There were three today, four if you count the one that made me cry, even more yesterday and the day before, but today's are fresh and magical. I think of telling Mark, but I've either had too many or too few drinks to articulate just how much I'm going to miss teaching.

I didn't plan on this after-work drink being so nostalgic, but it's Annalyse's fault. She said she had something to drop by during lunch. I forgot, of course. Kids say they'll be all kinds of places they never go, so I didn't wait. I kept teaching, and here she came into my class as if she belonged. She reached out and handed me a letter, a school picture attached, perfect spelling smattered with perfect handwriting, all meant to wreak havoc on my day.

"Please don't retire, so me and my friends can have you one more year," she says. "Jordyn and MoMo want you to stay too, so don't go."

This is the first time it occurred to me I wished I only taught eighth grade.

I can't blame her.

My eighth-grade classes are filled with more dynamic characters than any author could envision in any plot.

When Celina, the girl from the group home, finally arrived on Friday morning, a half hour into class, I had to ask if she'd ever read an entire book. It's polite to ask, but I hate asking.

"I read *The Hunger Games*," she said.

"But kids who can and do read *The Hunger Games* don't actually ditch class," I wanted to say but couldn't, knowing that finding a direct line of communication was not the best idea in this situation.

I thought of telling her I saw her walk by with Jesus the day before, letting her know her Chola-inspired eyeliner and carnage-red lipstick burned my eyes like a five-alarm fire in a five-gallon barrel, but I didn't.

"Didn't I see you in the hallway yesterday?" I said.

"I got checked out," she said.

At this point another kid might say, "Call my mom," the idea that Mom may continue coming to the rescue that reassuring or the idea of a teacher possibly following through on a threat of a phone call that improbable.

But Celina doesn't have a mom to call, and group homes don't carry the porbrecito gene. Getting "checked out" and reading *The Hunger Games* are her only weapons; her pencil-thin eyeliner is her shield of honor.

I turned to my sales team, students with dark pasts and bright futures, called them over one by one to convince Celina in one minute what took them days, weeks, or months to learn.

"I used to yell all the time."

"I didn't care about my grades."

"Dude, you'll like reading, I promise. Just do what she says."

They smiled, their faces radiating confidence and self-awareness.

"I was the worst—just ask Ms., but now my grades are up, I have respect from my parents and my teachers—it's cool; really, reading is cool. It changed me."

But Celina's brick walls and barbed wire wrapping made an impenetrable fortress.

My time was up.

"Well, you can grab something from my shelf or go to the library," I said, "or bring something from home if you want."

Same words, different tactic. With Abel I had to feign indifference to match his own, lull him in, hit him over the head when he thought I didn't care.

Celina is much more complicated.

I must feign confidence.

Eventually she gave into bringing something from home, but I know it won't happen. I just need to prepare for the next time I might see her, preparing for a tsunami just as easy and straightforward.

I tell Mark none of this, of course. I can't. I don't feel like crying.

"Cheers!" he says.

"Cheers to what?" I say.

"Cheers to you—you're about to retire, my friend."

We clink glasses.

This is not a celebration.

Today Araceli started reading *Perks of Being a Wallflower*.

She fake read *The Bully* until I stopped her. The life threatening summer accident on a quad that almost killed her, the subsequent concussion that snuck its way into the eighth grade slowed her down, burned her eyes, hurt her head, and lulled me into a passive bystander while she struggled with demons real and imagined.

I stared at her every day, fidgeting between the blue denim-jumper teacher on one shoulder and the deranged sabertooth on the other, fighting off the innate part of me that wanted to rip off her head and shove books into her gullet where they would wiggle and squirm until eventually, hopefully, blooming and flowering into their true potential.

But she had a concussion.

Woe is the teacher who must wait.

After two months I called her over, explained how a first book should be like a candy bar, a favorite candy bar, all gooey and crunchy and easy to chew and better to swallow. "This is not your candy bar," I said.

"It's fine," she said.

"Seriously, what's your favorite candy bar?" I said.

"Kit Kat," she said.

"I just don't believe this is your Kit Kat," I said as I set a copy of *Drive By* on top of the book she wasn't reading anyway. "Why don't you try this?" I said.

It might as well have been a piece of rotted meat, maggots wriggling to and fro, gangrene making its home in her tormented psyche.

She didn't speak, but her eyes began to well. I had no idea why.

"I just want you to try it," I said, back peddling out of this discomfort, the boundaries I may have just trampled causing me to question my tone, my motivation, my impulse.

Was I wrong to push her after so long?

Yes.

No.

Yes.

No.

She began to full-on bawl, tears streaming. By then I was even more and less adamant I had finally done the right thing by her.

"Just take it with you, and try it. If you don't like it, bring it back, and we'll try something else—we're just looking for the right candy bar," I said. "Really."

I'd never had a child react the way Araceli did, no one ever so obviously upset.

I had to be right.

But I could have been completely wrong.

I prayed that night to do no harm, to help, not to hinder.

Then next day she came in smiling. "Ask me about chapter one," she said.

No one ever throws down that challenge without knowing the answer.

The tears were gone, replaced by confidence and pride.

This morning, five months later, she asked for *Perks*. "Maria said it was good."

Mark knows this story, he knows the happy endings and changed lives, but there's one more, one more that has me wave the bartender over for another round.

I don't drink this much, I swear, but really, if you knew what

I knew, felt what I felt on a daily basis, you would see the heart can only take so much on any given day.

Today was that day.

Maggie and I are colleagues, sometimes text messengers, always emailers, occasional happy-hour participants.

But today, despite seeing her five times in the hallway and spending thirty minutes at lunch together, she never said a thing about *The Hate U Give* until I received an email ten minutes after she walked in and out of my room.

Before today I have often said the only people who know what I'm doing in 111 are the ones actually in there, but now Maggie knows.

I was kind and generous, and now she's mad.

But it's her fault.

She asked. She was young, looking for a friend and didn't have a book over the summer. "Here, take this," I said. She texted me when she finished: "Now what?"

I gave her *True Diary* and then *Always Running*, and she kept asking, so I kept giving.

And now she has me thinking of creating a little diagram of sorts, something to set down between Maslow's Hierarchy of Needs and Bloom's Taxonomy, a simplistic pictograph for anyone wondering what just happened to my friend.

But it wouldn't be a pyramid.

More like an ancient vine that starts in the pinky toe, serpentining its way through the unsuspecting, swallowing old ideas whole, leaving marks and scratches, new thoughts, new reasoning rendering readers helpless, their hearts and minds corrupted and disfigured by words they'd never imagined, aligned in such a way as to poke and prod and knock them unconsciously conscious.

I can only imagine this is what happened to Maggie. She

texted me from twenty feet away, no need to say in person what she could say in the safety of her own room.

She had just walked in and handed me *The Hate U Give* and told me she hated me.

"You want another one?" I said, reaching for Jason Reynolds's *All American Boys*. "I heard this was fantastic."

Admittedly, she looked upset. I thought she may need a hug, but I was teaching. Life was continuing.

She walked out.

Ten minutes later my phone vibrated.

> I keep thinking about the book. And how I'm not doing enough. And why. And how I never had a talk with my parents when I was twelve about what to do or what not to do around police. And how I'm not afraid of getting pulled over.

> But that's not even why I'm mad at you right now. 'Cause then I'm thinking about how I brought the book back to you and was mad at you and grateful at the same time. And then you go and hand me another one. And as I walk out in the hall, a kid goes, "She's feeding you books too," then I realize that you've been playing me like the kids this whole time. Except instead of being the book pusher who's trying to save my life with books, you're pushing other ones that'll help me save more lives and now I can't decide if I hate you for leaving us or love you for feeding me books and teaching me things that transcend beyond the classroom.

> So there.

I hold my phone out with the text on the screen. Mark takes it, makes some sounds, nods his head, but I'm not looking at him.

Eye contact and tequila do not mix.

"I know what she's talking about," he says. "You did the same thing to me with *Coldest Winter*, remember?

Of course I remember. Mark had walked into a classroom of potential hooligans, looked around, and said, "I know these guys—what did you do to them?"

The boy who found the blow job on page three was in that class, a room full of kids Mark had been struggling to help, no idea I was meddling in their business as well. He assured me, "I don't read."

That night, I called my own dealer, the friend, the colleague, the teacher who had fueled my burgeoning book collection. "What do I give a middle-aged man?"

Three weeks later, the games on the television sets at Hooter's were not to his liking. A cold beer in his hand, a bed full of fries and a burger at arm's reach, his friends speechless as he took *The Coldest Winter* out of his gym bag, the moist red lips on the cover taunting his buddies to heckle and harass him.

I'd pay money to have heard that conversation.

The Hooter's incident spurred the I Got Caught Club, and my kids began to tell the stories about the first time their parents saw them reading without being told.

"She asked if I was on drugs," someone said.

"He asked me where my phone was," said someone else.

"'Are you in trouble?'"

"'Does your mother know you've been reading?'"

"That story never gets old," I tell Mark.

It's midnight by the time we go our separate ways. We

started early but tapered off toward the end, no need to nurse a Saturday-morning hangover at our age.

By Sunday my end-of-the-year angst has dissipated, but the endlessly closed library and the book-juggling from my classroom shelves has exacerbated what I will have to do for the next few weeks.

School-teacher dreams this time of the year are almost always about control: bladder control, shopping-cart control, bank-account control, carnival rides gone awry.

But this Sunday-night dream is not a horror-filled nightmare of me standing in front of the class nude, lesson-plan-less, trying desperately to hold water or sand or grains of rice in my hands, everything slipping through despite my useless attempts to close my fingers together and palm what is left before the wind comes...

Nope. None of those are my dream, but I've had those dreams more times than I'd like to admit.

A teacher's dream is a view through an orgasmic Freudian psychotic kaleidoscope, proving once and for all, dreams are our way of processing our lives. Without dreams there would be an entire unit in the psychiatric ward dedicated to middle school personnel.

In this dream I make a friend. We're neighbors. He stops by and we chat and it goes on for few months, talking here, talking there, conversations about the weather, the news, the day-to-day, and then one day, I don't know how, as it is with dreams, I end up on his street.

We live in back-to-back cul-de-sacs, literally a hundred yards from one another, but it seems I'd never been down his street, never visited him at his place; he always came to my house.

Then one day I'm out for a walk, and I look over and realize it is Henry's house. Maybe I knew the address or the design, I don't really know why I know, but I just know, this is Henry's house. But it's not really Henry, as dreams go. I don't really know his name.

I look at the front door, and I think of the people he's mentioned coming and going from his house and wonder how they all would fit in such a tiny place, and then I look up and wonder how can I still be in Tucson.

Henry's house, right behind my tiny, normal-sized house, is an impressive brownstone apartment towering above me, so massive it's blocked out the sun.

I go inside.

As it happens I have no idea how I get into the actual apartment, but I'm there in the living room taking notes amid works of art hung on the wall, fancy furniture more at home in a New York apartment than a Tucson rental, explaining to all the passers-by, "I'm friends with Henry."

They nod and smile, these friends and family members of Henry. They all have that sort of smile that says sure, we understand you don't belong here, no need to explain; we already knew that.

After a few minutes, a little girl comes into the room; she's no more than nine. I can't see her face, I can't tell you what she's doing, I don't remember talking to her. Eventually though something happens. I remember her eating something, licking something, a book maybe? Maybe two books?

The adults come as expected. What did you do; what did you eat? What happened to you, little girl?

She tries to explain. "I licked the book."

No one seems to know why a little girl would lick a book or two books or more even, but it would also seem the book was not poisonous. The worst thing that will happen is the little girl will suffer a stomachache, she'll be fine, no rush to the hospital for little Suzie, also not her real name. Dreams are like that, nameless children, harmless book licking.

Finally, an adult asks Susie—the little girl more apt to be in a Jane Austen novel or the main character in *Atonement* than my classroom anywhere at any time in MUSD—why she licked the book. Everyone seems to be waiting for the answer.

She's only nine, little Susie, but she has the answer, and she's being taken seriously, like there is some reasonable reason as to why someone would lick a book. Everyone wants to know, I want to know, I'm there in the living room, I'm the narrator and the silent observer and I too want to know, why Susie, why lick a book?

But I didn't speak. I didn't ask her; someone else asked her, but she looks at me—right at me.

"Choices," she says. "Choices."

And then she smirks.

She smirks like only a snotty little girl from the top floor of a Manhattan brownstone with two little poodles and one hairless Chihuahua with a Salvadoran maid and a Chinese cook and a mink winter coat and a spring wardrobe can smirk.

And what's that behind her?

The fuzzy wall behind her smirky little face?

A library.

An entire wall devoted to words.

She can do what she wants.

She can choose.

I want to grab her by the earlobe—and then, in an instant, I wake up.

That little snot has choices.

Choices, I think.

Choices.

15

TESTING POSITIVE

I heard William Golding had no real plan when he wrote *Lord of the Flies*. He merely wanted to find out what would happen if a bunch of boys were stranded on an island together.

It's quite possible his research began and ended on the first day of spring in a middle school—no need to look further to find chaos, anarchy, and the loss of morality. If he needed a week's worth of material, then he need only refer to the state's testing window to find the best time to observe.

It's not like Christmas or a birthday. I believe the date is arbitrary. I wouldn't know; I just give the test when I'm told to give the test. The state's test administrators seem unconcerned by the fact we're giving finals six weeks before we can cover all the material.

But what am I saying? Of course the state doesn't care.

During the week, Cruella and I write bored Haikus back and forth to show our commitment to the necessity of four hours of silent bubbling.

Advice from Yoda
"There is no try, only do …"
Just write something down!

Prepared they are not
We made a plan for the wind
But then came the rain

Standardized testing
School's way of proving that we
Differentiate

Ridiculous test
Annoying in every way
When will it all end?

But we know when this test ends, it takes four days for the students to write an essay and answer approximately seventy questions in math and reading. Somehow we spread these four days into five and ruin an entire week of school.

Not to mention closing down the library indefinitely while make-up testing occurs. Students like Celina and Manny with sporadic attendance get roped and tied into a seat if they come for even a second during the testing window.

Certainly there are children who could finish the entire test in one day and move on with their lives, but not here in the land of testing, where the week's activities are as archaic as the technology behind the answering …

Tech essay assigned
Tech passages to read
Tech used? The pencil.

We aren't supposed to look at the test, not copy it, repeat it, blab about it, tell Soviet spies about it, or let it get into unsupervised hands, but right away on day one, just twenty minutes into testing, a student walks up with his bubble sheet in hand.

Due to coordination reasons, this child is not one on my roster, but I'm giving him his test, and this is important to note since his entire test, all four days of it, is done.

"When did you do this?" I ask.

"Friday in the library," he says.

In more than ten ways this is a serious breach of testing protocol. Who knows how many kids he's talked to about the test over the weekend. All the questions and the answers and the secrets are probably all out on the internet as we speak. Oh, the horror! The embarrassment of the explanation! The blame! The accusation!

Plus, I don't know if he's lying or telling the truth. Maybe he just bubbled the shit out of the test just now and I didn't notice. I only know he's done and no one should be done anywhere in the entire school.

"We just started," I say. "Who gave you the test?"

"I don't know," he says. "Some lady in the library."

"What lady?" I say.

"That one with the hair," he says.

I flip through the teacher's guide for protocol that may cover this mistake in judgment, colossal break in continuity, egregious error in—I could go on and on, possibly do a string of alliterations with Maggie—but as for now, I find nothing in the protocol with which to beat this child.

I'm not cheating, I swear, and I have no intention or desire to infiltrate the Arizona State Standardized Testing Organization, but I have to look through this test to figure out what went wrong when, completely accidentally, without even trying, four words catch my eye: *West with the Night*.

Illegally, against every oath I've ever taken, I skim the passage.

The three-paragraph excerpt, arguably written by Hemingway if not one of the most unrecognized yet notable female writers of her time, Beryl Markham, is being used as a reading passage for seventh graders.

Why stop at Markham? Why not try a little Tolstoy or Dostoyevsky or Dickens?

I look at the clock. We've only been testing for twenty-seven minutes. I do the math. If all goes well, I'll only be testing kids for another three and a half hours, plenty of time to lose my entire mind and not just the twenty-seven minutes of it I've lost so far.

West with the Night? Why? Who could possibly think this was an option for a seventh-grade test?

How did I not see this?

This isn't about testing; it's not about understanding our students' ability in reading or math. It's about classifying our children into categories, giving them a ceiling, a roof above their heads into which they can knock themselves unconscious.

It's obvious now. The vocational and academic tracts we say we discontinued continue.

I look around the room and see such sincerity in their effort. I want to tell them, "Hey! It's a lie! This doesn't test your ability. It classifies you, categorizes you, puts you in a box the likes of which you cannot escape!"

I must warn everyone.

I must.

But no one will hear. They'll say it's a conspiracy, and I'll say, "Yes! It's a conspiracy!" But they won't get it.

It is a conspiracy.

I thought, all this time I thought—no, I believed—I actually believed we were testing to see how well they read and completed math and then we'd use those scores to teach.

We spend hours and hours of professional development discussing *data*, looking at *data*, talking about *data*, deciding which kids need interventions in which areas in order to improve test scores.

We're also told every year never to look at the tests. Anything I've ever seen before was just in a glance, but this discovery means so much more, and I only know this because I've read this particular beautiful, beautiful book.

I always thought they didn't want us cheating, skipping ahead, finding questions about theme and spoon-feeding those ideas so our children could pass parts of the test.

Now I know they didn't want us to know it's all a scam.

Meanwhile everyone's head is down, pencils are moving, there's no yawning, no stretching, just focused attention, except the kid who's finished, he's coloring a pretty little Care Bear.

Today I get a potty break whenever I need. I need one now, not to really pee but to purge.

I wait until one of my students needs to use the restroom, and I whisper to him to ask one of the hallway testing monitors to cover my classroom.

I wish it were a Xanax break, though, like an old-school cig-arette break without all the smoke inhalation. Maybe we could have a Xanax dispenser? Prozac? Any antidepressant would do. I'm thinking about the pharmaceutical companies and the cash they would make with a teachers' lounge, antidepressant vending machine in every school across the United States.

I look in the mirror while I'm there, note the white hair, not-so-white teeth, the portrait of a teacher at the end of her career, so many stories of children gone awry I could spend a lifetime telling stories of woe—woe is me; woe is them.

I think about really getting into it, owning my own misery, my career gone by, so many mistakes I could fill a bathtub or a pool, potentially one Olympic in size.

But I can't hide in the bathroom all day.

Surely, they would send a search party.

As I shuffle back to class, preparing myself for four more days, saying, "You can color silently while those around you finish," or, "You can work on a dot to dot," or, "You can put your head down and sleep," I fantasize another world where I run down the hall, screaming, "It's a lie! It's all a lie!"

My arms flailing, teachers and children poking their heads out of their rooms wondering what happened to poor Ms. Russell, the teacher who went cray-cray during testing week and never quite made it to her retirement party.

By the afternoon I feel better, nothing like four white walls to subdue the anarchist in me. Our schedules are back to normal, our testing materials locked away in the library, an armed guard in front, an armored tank outside just in case the Russians want access to our testing materials, maybe change right answers to wrong, blow another hole in our deflated egos.

Wednesday we still have our professional development with Pacheco's rundown of the failures and successes of the week. He reiterates the importance of attendance this week and says the eighth graders are beating out the sixth and seventh graders for the possibility of having free dress on Friday.

"Free dress," I whisper to Maggie. "It's going to be a freak show—doesn't he know it's spring? Everyone is going to try to break the dress code all day, and he won't have enough room in in-house for any of them."

"Can't wait to see the tube tops and spaghetti straps," she says.

"My favorite is the short-shorts," I say, the least controlled piece of clothing in the spring ensemble of a teenager.

By Friday all has spiraled. The anxiety of being locked away for five days and the anticipation of three hundred teenagers wearing whatever they want has taken its toll on the students as well as the teachers, and any semblance of order I had been maintaining in class has begun to fray.

Students who were five feet tall on Monday are six feet tall by Friday, twenty-five kids feel like thirty-five, and even though there aren't actual flying planes and soaring wads of spit, my skin and my psyche feel as though an entire football game was played right here in my room every day all day for a week. The players, the band, and the bystanders played in my head, popcorn and sticky stains of candy and soda pop lay scattered, every step on the linoleum comes with the *crunch* and *shtick* on the soles of my shoes.

I feel like the off-duty police officer in front of the Black Friday doors of any store with chaotic potential.

Differentiating between the ones who want to barrel down the door and the ones who just want to pick up a few bargain deals is an internal battle that makes me uneasy and angry at the same time.

A student plays with the snaps on his shorts—snap on, snap off, snap on and off—over and over again.

Tap, tap, tap of a pencil in the back.

A basketball under an unconscious foot squeaks with every move back and forth, back and forth across the ball.

One person sneezes, and a chorus of "bless yous" fills the room, half continue reading, half start giggling.

I had to enforce silent reading so I didn't have a meltdown.

A group is still giggling.

"Zip it, people," I say. "We can chill after we chill."

I say this because I plan on letting them just chill, but they won't.

My classes are not the kind where you can tell them all to talk freely and they just talk freely. Instead one wadded-up paper becomes a one-on-one basketball game, a bump into each other becomes a wrestling match, one person at the drinking fountain becomes five, phones come out, headphones come out, everyone talks louder than they've ever talked before, the basketball comes out and starts to bounce magically, as if there hasn't been an anti-bouncing-ball policy since day one, something flies across the room, and then something else.

My second period is the last class of the day. I don't know why. I'm not the testing coordinator, and I've never volunteered to be one, but now a class I normally love might as well all be standing at the chalkboard with fifty sets of hands with five fingernails each scraping away.

I look up at the clock.

It's not moving.

It's in the same place it was five minutes ago.

Is that possible?

It's not moving, is it?

I hear yelling from the bathroom.

Yelling from the hallway.

Some of my colleagues have given into the pressure, too many students allowed at once to the bathroom, and chaos begins to ooze out of the rooms into the hallway.

A college student walks outside under my classroom window with his stereo blasting a rap song everyone in the room seems to know but me.

Monday seems so long ago.

Destiny walks over and sits on my stool.

"Oh," I say. "I didn't notice your new look."

"You like?" she says.

I don't know how I didn't notice, but she has a green mustache drawn across her top lip, blue sideburns down her cheeks, and a tiny black goatee drawn in with what appears to be permanent marker.

"Interesting," I say.

"It's Rainbow Day in the book I'm reading."

Of course it is, I think, along with, shit—I have to ask Mark what happened. I make a mental note to email him when Destiny says, "Did you hear? I'm back with my mom."

"Oh, that's great," I lie, because we lie all the time. "When did that happen?"

"Today is the first day," she says.

"Of course it is," I say. "That's why the Rainbow Day celebration makes so much sense," and why emailing Mark is now unnecessary.

"Exactly," says my little friend, the butterfly, as she flitters back to her seat.

Even her feet gently touching the ground sounds like tiny rockets exploding inside my head.

I sit in my chair and rock, check my email, look at the clock, look at the simmering water before me, look back up at the clock.

Abel walks up.

"Can I drop off something at the office?" he says.

"Drop off what?" I say.

"Oh nothing," he says as he slips out the door.

He has papers in his hands when he returns, and I can't help but ask him what they are. I threaten him with detentions, F grades, and grounding.

"You can't ground me," he says.

"I can try," I say, and then I just start begging.

"Okay, okay," he says. "Well, I want to help my mom out, you know? With bills and stuff—she does a lot—there's a lot of kids in my house."

"I can't even imagine," I say, and I can't. I cannot comprehend a brood of tiny Abels running around a house. How could anyone ever have enough money to feed more than one child much less interact and parent and love a whole herd?

"They have a teen program with the county—you hear of it?"

Of course I have.

A government agency hires kids from fourteen to eighteen years of age for cleanup crews on the streets of Tucson or custodian work in the schools or food distribution at the Food Bank, every job an opportunity to put some money in a kid's front pockets for now, some pride and ownership in their back pockets for later, when they are older and need to be reminded of their successes and their value.

"Pacheco told me to come by and pick up an application," he says.

I'd spend some time getting happy about Abel and his summer job, even about Pacheco reaching out to a child, such a long way from the usual crossed-arm pose he uses to keep students and teachers at a distance, but teachers don't have time for happiness and celebrations. Sure, Abel might want a job, but that doesn't prevent him from dropping out and doing drugs and following Jesus down whatever nasty hole that boy may have fallen.

After the testing materials are locked away in the library and all the students are all shooed off campus for the weekend, I check my email one last time before leaving.

Seven messages down from a slew of educational sites wanting me to buy books and go back to school and ignite my classroom and achieve higher test scores, there's a "JO" in a subject line followed by an email from Rodriguez stating Jesus Olivas was caught simulating a sexual hand gesture toward her student teacher.

"Vigorously," she writes.

Choices.

Some better than others.

In 2014 I checked my retirement account daily for two weeks after two years with multiple students who blasted the same theme song. "It Wasn't Me" blaring from the earphones they weren't wearing, sagging in the pants they weren't sagging, spewing from their mouths when they weren't even talking.

"Why are you in in-house?"

"He got me in trouble."

"Why are you in in-house?"

"She was messing with my—"

"Why are you in in-house?"

"I don't know. I didn't do nothing."

Of course you didn't.

You never do.

When we call home on those kids, it's the same sad story over and over: "Sorry, ma'am, your child has a terrible case of apple-and-the-tree syndrome."

Our condolences.

"Remember that year?" I say to Maggie. "Oh, wait, you were still in grade school—my bad."

It was the year a girl bit a boy on the cheek and the bite mark remnants lasted five days longer than the biter's punishment.

"I may not have been here for that, but I remember when that boy threw his desk across the room—wait," she says. "Didn't you throw the same desk across the room to show his grandparents what he did?"

"Maybe," I say, but I did. It was a glorious demonstration in front of seven educators, my principal, and the grandparents, complete silence in the room as I grabbed the back of the chair and flipped over the entire desk set, sending it sliding across the floor and into the wall just like their little pookie had done three days prior.

Thousands of stories of misbehavior, misadventure, lessons gone awry, outbursts of anger, thoughts of quitting, leaving, walking right out the door, never to return. Thousands of thoughts flitter-flap in my head.

Choices.

This week alone there are at least five stories of naughty shenanigans, six if you count the kid with the free porn access in one of our computer labs. Seven if you count Jesus's interpretation of a hands-on activity.

I choose not to tell those stories.

The world needs to know for every one cheek-biting, desk thrower there are a thousand Abels.

Instead of heading home, I head for Pacheco's office. He's never the last to leave the parking lot, but he also is never the first.

I tap gently on his doorframe. We do get along. I just trash talk the part of him that acquiesces to bully parents and conniving kids. His job is part bouncer and part New York City detective, just not the strong parts.

"Long week, eh?" I say.

"Could have gone smoother, that's for sure—what's up?"

"Oh, I just wanted to thank you for getting that application for Abel," I say.

"Sorry," he says. "I don't know what you're talking about—Abel Cazares? Haven't seen him."

I explain to him how Abel came to get the job application, how Pacheco tapped him, told him about it, encouraged him to apply.

"He said you told him he could put you down as a reference," I say.

"He did? That's funny because all that happened is he came in asking about the county jobs and I didn't know anything about it, so I sent him to Mr. Scott—that's the last I heard from him."

"But he said you're helping him—you aren't helping him?"

"No, he came to me. I just told him where to go."

No matter how many times I say what I'm trying to say, he doesn't seem to get why I cannot comprehend what Abel did. It's so simple, though, so obvious now that I've said it over and over again to Abel's only alibi.

Abel is a liar.

16

BARRY CALLED

Even without the end-of-the-year Celinas passing through, we already spend eight hours a day in a permanent state of metacognition, constant brain chatter filled with backstory. Did I do this right? Am I doing this right? Should I do this differently? Are my lessons on my desk? Is my objective on the board? Will I be evaluated today or tomorrow or next week? Do I have enough paper, enough pencils?

Do we still have those shitty pencils?

We may be on the job for eight or nine hours, but we are teachers twenty-four hours a day, even when we are out sick, even when we take a mental-health day, rain or shine, Christmas break or Easter.

Summer break?

It's just a long weekend.

My dad still tells stories, and he's been retired for fifteen years.

"Did I tell you about that guy—I don't know what he said, but he said somethin' to this girl, and she grabbed him by the face like that." He puts his hand up like a claw too. "And then by the throat with the other hand and practically lifted that sucker off the ground!" he says, his voice rising while he laughs.

"Next day he's wearin' his Sunday best." My dad's southern drawl is a little more south than people are used to hearing. "I mean best slacks, best jacket, and best tie—graduated top of his class—he's superintendent of some district in Denver." He pauses a bit. I used to think it was because he was so worked up about his story, but I was wrong.

He's been a storyteller since I've known him.

Despite being able to tell at least three stories a day for the last twenty-nine years, being able to cast a light on the daily on some of America's darkest shadows, I still can't beat my dad.

"D'I ever tell you about that girl who—" every single time I see him.

"'Bout that boy who wrote the essay so he could go to the NBA game?"

"The one about that girl who became chief petty officer?"

The pharmacist?

The mechanic?

Yes, Dad. You have. Plenty of times. But that's okay. Tell me again.

These are my thoughts as Celina slinks through the doorway right past me and toward the back of my class.

Years ago the eighth-grade team had another group-home girl. When Mr. Scott took her on a school tour and offered her some school supplies, he said she reached for the ballpoint pens, pulled off the caps, and put the pens back into his hand. "They're good for smoking weed," she told him.

By seventh period five boys reported being propositioned.

Years later PenCap still holds the gold standard for group-home girls, but as Celina surveys my room, I'm wondering if she may eclipse PenCap.

When class starts I sit at my desk before I call her over.

I'm a zookeeper with a brand-new leopard on the grounds,

twenty antelope running free, and I have to teach everybody how to play nicey-nice or I will lose an antelope a day.

"Hey," I say as I point to the stool.

She looks around the room as she walks, taking a seat as if it were center stage.

"Can I see your schedule?" I say.

I don't really care about her schedule; I just want to see how she's doing, how we're doing, what's happened in the ten days since we spoke.

She pulls a paper out of her backpack and thrusts it at me, and now it seems pretty clear she doesn't even remember meeting me.

I don't react to her anger. I'd be mad too if I had had a life that led me to the home where she's been assigned, my childhood filled with peach trees and pumpkin pie compared to this girl's. Instead I hold the paper carefully, looking at it seriously as if I'm not really cursing Pacheco for giving Celina the same schedule he gave Manny.

Of course, his plan is to protect the antelope, but what he forgets is we also have to help the leopards.

I hand back her schedule and give her a shortened version of my why-we-read lecture.

She cuts me off halfway and says, "I don't read."

I don't say, "They didn't either," like I did with Abel. These are not her peers.

"Well, you can look on the shelf at the books I have, or you can write me an essay about who you are, how you ended up at Mission Heights—stuff like that."

"I'll get a book," she says as if we have met, a thousand times, and all those times still grate on her, the teachers in her head like all the other adults she knows.

I watch her as she walks away, reaches out to the bookshelf, and just like those adults, no discerning between good and bad, she grabs a book as if they are also all the same.

Within minutes I hear people asking about her four-hour day. "Why do you only have four classes? You must be really good in school," someone says.

"You have straight As?" someone says. "You must have straight As."

Celina laughs. "No," she says.

"Let's go ahead and start with silent reading, people," I say.

I take attendance and check my email while surveying the room for readers, side eyeing my new student but not making eye contact. Her mood has changed. Ten days of bad decisions has set us backward, and we hadn't even moved forward.

But one of my students keeps looking at Celina, apparently quite moved by her pronouncement of her four-hour schedule. An invisible hierarchy has been established, this girl's gravitation pulling my student away from me and into her.

My anger with Ed flares again.

Someone really should study what happens when a perfectly fine garden has a healthy morning glory nestled down into the ground right next to the primroses, daffodils, and dandelions.

Wait. There have been studies.

My bad.

Morning glories are beautiful but need to be watched, trimmed, and meticulously tended lest they weave and wind their way around, stretching and searching for the perfect place to catch all the sun's rays, while the prized petunias and the pink peonies are left sunless.

Celina's hand gestures make no sense to me, but this is a dangerous alliance. This particular student Celina has chosen is just two weeks out of her latest suspension for celebrating 4/20 at school on the nation's unofficial marijuana-inspired holiday.

If I'm not vigilant, she may be caught in the bathroom again with a pen cap.

The 152 days I started out with Abel seem like a million in comparison to the number we have left, Celina and I.

Class ends with the titter of kids enjoying the find of a new best friend as I walk back to the back row, where Celina left the book unopened and upside down.

As her class leaves and Diego's enters, I'm grateful Celina is not in fifth period, back-to-back tsunamis much more manageable than twins.

"Where's your collared shirt?" I say as he passes by hoodless, earphone-less.

He says he forgot.

"I'll just go tell Pete," he says.

"Diego," I say, "do you always have to go to Pacheco? Can't you be like a normal kid for once and just go find the monitor?"

"A'ight," he says as he walks out, casually, carefree, like he has great relationships with everyone and Pacheco's his rich uncle.

We're responsible when we send out students like Diego, our reputations relying on the life choices of fourteen-year-old boys.

Once I had a principal who blamed teachers' lesson plans for the lack of student engagement and thus the abundance of student misbehavior at the school. According to the worst principal I ever had, that's why little Johnny fought and got high and had low self-esteem and stole $10,000 of audio/visual equipment.

Diego is destined to mouth off to some adult who takes offense to his sagging pants and careless gait.

"Whatcha doing, boy? Ain't you got nowhere to be?"

Million to one he doesn't answer, "I am on my way to find the monitor so I can get a uniform shirt."

I perseverate while he's gone, to the point someone asks, "Are you nervous you let Diego out?"

"No," I tell them. "I'm just in a bad mood."

But when Diego walks back into class, the same kid says, "I told you," and I just want to smack him.

"How'd it go?" I ask Diego.

"Fine, but now my shirt is rachety."

This presents an entirely new issue. The school rule is specific: solid blue or solid white sweatshirts only.

But we're also told to pick our battles.

"Walk up to Rodriguez and politely ask if you could wear it for a day. Be honest; tell her what happened," I say, as casually as possible, my insides a testament to internal combustion, the bright pink of Diego's sweatshirt burning my eyes.

"I'll just go to Pacheco," he says, and just as I open my mouth to scream, he says, "Just kidding. I'll ask."

I grab the phone the second he walks out the door. Freaking kid. I don't want his face ripped off and fed to the cubs.

I can't tell Rodriguez what to do, but I can give her a choice, suggest she may ignore a pink sweatshirt in light of a student politely asking a favor.

Either way they are both likely to say the same thing, "Eff you. I'm going to Pacheco."

I make my call and follow the stragglers into the hallway.

In the amount of time most of the world takes to walk over to the office water cooler, fill their cup, and sip leisurely, basking in the glow of downtime, I say hi to ten kids, head nod two adults, peek in Maggie's room to see her still on the computer, give five slide-handshake-knuckle-bumps, have six kids ask me for food, have one ask me if I know what a "fag" is, yell, "Hey!"

at three different students for cussing, yell at five more hanging by our own water cooler, and then hug three more as they pass by on their way to someone else's class.

"Hey," Maggie says as she pops out seconds before the bell rings.

"You sound weird," I say.

"Weiss just sent out an email," she says.

"Don't tell me. She wants the whole eighth grade retained because they aren't ready 'for the demands of high school.'"

"Well, you got half of it right," she says. "But it's not the whole school; it's just Abel."

I turn and see Maria with her seventh-grade boyfriend in the hallway. They're hugging, not quite kissing, but probably only because they know normally I'll yell, "I love you, I love you, I love you," over and over until they stop kissing in my hallway.

Her boyfriend is a seventh grader. I've checked his grades, and they aren't like Maria's. The fact he's in Mark's room sometimes and Maria is never in there makes me even crazier, and right now after hearing about Weiss's new hunting spree, no one is safe.

"Maria, come here," I say.

She looks scared, and she should be.

"A seventh grader?" I used to tease her.

"Isn't he like eleven years old?" I used to taunt her, but now I'm more pointed.

I don't know why I'm like this, but I can't stop myself.

By now there's no one in the hallway, and my next class is my planning period, so I have plenty of time to tell Maria what I think of her boyfriend.

"I see you're still dating Kyle," I say. "If you had a daughter, would you let her date him?"

She shakes her head back and forth.

"Then if you wouldn't let your daughter date him, you shouldn't either." I walk into my class and grab a piece of paper on the table by the door. She follows me into the room.

I lean over and start writing.

"I know this doesn't make sense," I say, "but she'll date the exact kind of boys you date, so who you date now matters later."

I hand her the piece of paper.

She looks down.

"It's a bookmark," I say.

I matter. I'm important. I'm worthy of more.

I take the paper back.

Homework: Say these three lines in the mirror three times and then ask yourself, "Should I stay, or should I go?"

I show this to her. She nods her head, and then I write one more line.

I love Maria, but Maria has to love Maria too.

I draw a heart and sign my name.

"I'm serious," I say.

"I know," she says.

When she leaves I look around the room, see what other tables I can overturn, see my shelf of books is getting low, and I don't know exactly how to judge this turnaround time. If someone else like Gero finishes right now, it is doubtful he'll have enough time for a final book, but I can't give him free time, but I can't give him something he can't finish, but I can't make him give a book back, but I can't give away more books that won't be returned.

I look at my desks. They're out of alignment and dirty. The floor has Takis and pencils and scraps of paper, and it looks like someone had a tiny torn eraser fight I didn't notice in the last class.

I start cleaning.

I have an hour before my last class of the day, and I need some semblance of order before I even dare to look at that email.

"Barry Manilow called," says Maggie.

"What? No way." I'm fully focused now. I love me some "Copacabana," and I feel a little better after my cleaning spree.

"He offered MUSD a piano."

"No way. Really? What did we say?"

"'No thanks.'"

I stand in awe.

"Don't blame me," she says as she kicks up her door holder and begins to shut her door. "I just work here."

It's hard not to think about MUSD's gross negligence, but I have to stay focused. One lapse in judgment and the whole place will catch on fire as we enter the end-of-the-year spiral.

"Take out your books, people," I say as I walk in my door. I need them started, moving toward reading, not asking me a thousand questions like why would anyone turn down a free piano.

I fantasize about a desk job sans thirteen-year-olds. I could go for a walk around the building, take up cigarettes and then have a cigarette break, walk outside for a drink of water at my leisure, pee when I want, even poop at work without worrying about thirty kids inside or outside of my classroom doing who-knows-what. If my boss was really flexible, I could get in my car and drive to Starbucks, do some yoga stretches, tai chi postures...if only Google needed reading teachers.

I pull out my calendar, mark off the days we've completed, assess the days we have left, determine whether to mark today off or leave it on, and look at the clock—2:50. I mark it off.

I need to know exactly how many more steps there are in this marathon.

I count slowly, one square at a time. I back up and count again.

I check my math one more time.

Twenty-two days.

I got this.

I'm positive.

I think.

17

BUTTERFLY KISSES

*"Of all the preposterous assumptions of humanity over humanity,
nothing exceeds most of the criticisms made on the habits of the
poor by the well-housed, well-warmed, and well-fed."*
—HERMAN MELVILLE

As I walk through the teacher workroom, I see Weiss on her pedestal. If she were sitting any higher, her tiara might just scrape the ceiling. "If you're not a little bit embarrassed by the teacher you used to be," she announces to one of our colleagues, "then you're probably doing something wrong."

I grab my mail and keep walking.

Embarrassment is for dangling boogers and blood-stained pants.

While other professions maintain continual forward momentum, enlightened ideas sustained and evolutionary, education swings comfortably on a pendulum.

Teachers know if we hold on long enough and tight enough the pendulum will swing back by and pick us up.

A school district in Iowa recently jumped on an old-school form of discipline by adopting enclosed time-out rooms with locks on the outside to hold unruly children.

The funding is questionable. Why would the state pay for

such an atrocity when they could just put the little suckers in the cafeteria walk-in freezer?

Fun four-letter words about Weiss continue to mumble their way past my lips as I pass through the courtyard and return to my room. I pull up my email, of course, and a whole new slew of words come raging out.

Weiss has set a new date for Manny's retention meeting.

My issue now is I can't decide to press *reply to all* or tell her to her face she already missed Manny's hanging.

I walk over to the drawer where Manny's book lays, pull it out, and walk back to my desk to set it down. I look at the cover. It's beautiful really, a tattooed man holding his baby in his arms, a photograph of poetic genius, a legacy in paperback.

Maggie walks in to grab something off the printer, and I say, "Do you think the government purposely doesn't want our children to think?"

"What have you been smoking?" says Maggie. "It's not even eleven o'clock. Are you high? Seriously?"

"One of my girlfriends used to call me a bouncy rubber ball. Is that what you mean?"

"Sort of. You do have a tendency to change topics."

"Manny's gone," I say.

I've been counting.

Today is day eleven of the Manny Disappearing Act, the day after students are dropped from MUSD. A student returning after a ten-day drop is as likely as the state of education becoming a national priority.

After I got him to read his first book, he was never late, never rude. He was considerate, purposeful, and respectful, but apparently only in my class.

In order to alleviate class preparedness, he kept his book in the cabinet next to his desk, no backpack required, his book never forgotten. If he ended up with Mark for any length of time, he just came over and picked up his book, read with Mark, and returned it.

Tyrell and *Bronxwood*, *The Absolutely True Diary of a Part-Time Indian*, and *Always Running* were all part of his personal library. He was reading Luis J. Rodriguez's follow-up memoir to *Running*, *It Calls You Back*, but he hadn't finished.

The last time I saw Manny, he'd just gotten off the bus, and he was walking toward the cafeteria. We both did a head nod, but he never arrived at my room. I found out later he told the principal he didn't feel well, so el jefe called his mom and told her he was on his way back home.

That was it.

Triage done, the patient bandaged, IV saline-solution drip added, vitamins and nutrients sent straight into the bloodstream.

In the end he pulled out all the cords and walked out of the hospital.

"Like he ditched and went to Circle K?"

"No, like he was dropped yesterday."

"Oh," says Maggie. "You knew this would happen, right? I didn't have him, but I kind of assumed this was going to happen, didn't you?"

"Yeah, I guess so."

There's no direct mention of Abel in Weiss's email. For this I'm grateful. It's hard to balance my emotional state with teacher cage fights in my head—insults abound, apples hurled, chalk flung, Weiss and I in opposite corners ready to throw down.

Well, I'm ready to throw down. I'm not so sure about her.

In class I oscillate around the room, making sure we're still reading. We have to still be reading; my sanity depends on it. I used to read silently while they read—some teaching guru suggested our children need models—but I looked unavailable to my students. If I'm busy they can't ask for vocabulary definitions and comprehension clarification. I'm a translator of sorts, helping my students maintain their relationships with books.

It's important to note Gero is hip deep in some present-day *Romeo and Juliet* when Isabel walks up with the second book in the *Perfect Chemistry* series.

"Finished," she says.

"I'll take that," Gero says as he grabs the book back off my desk.

"Dude, where did you come from?" I say. "You were just—"

"I've been waiting for this book—I need this book—I'm almost done with the first one."

"Almost done? I just gave you that one."

"I've been reading at home, Ms. I swear I'll finish before school's out."

My slack jaw goes unnoticed as the boy-who-wouldn't-read walks away, almost tripping while he reads the back cover on the way to his seat.

Isabel and I look at each other and laugh.

Gero.

"I didn't know you were reading *Rules of Attraction*. How'd that even happen?" I say.

"Abel," she says. "But I'm also more than halfway through *All American Boys.*"

"Ah," I say, but only because I don't know what to say. I have no idea how many books this boy has read behind my back, and now he has Maria reading behind my back as well. I've never met a group of more untrustworthy children.

A study conducted at the University of Nevada reported that the number of books in a home has a greater effect on a child's school success than a father's education level.

I wonder what this study would say about Abel or Isabel or even Manny for that matter.

I have to find a way to continue pushing books.

Abel is sitting in front of my desk, and he seems completely oblivious to his name being mentioned. He has a pencil in his hand, but I can't quite see what he's doing.

"How long you been reading that?" I say.

"I don't know," he says, without looking up, still marking.

It occurs to me his reading has slowed. This book not played like a lead guitar in a punk rock band, but savored more like the solo in a blues ballad.

And what is he doing with the pencil?

I look around at the remaining thirty students in his class. I could explain how each and every child is or is not progressing, but it's too much. They aren't rocks to be classified, diseases to identify. They are the flora and the fauna in an unadulterated forest, a microcosm at the bottom of an unobserved ocean, a newly discovered microbiome.

They are so complicated in the middle of their journeys, some ahead, some behind, some irritating the shit out of me with their low-brow apathy.

Not really. Well, yes, but only for the lack of effort. I have never come to terms with students who do not try; do not at least get out their pencil, get out their paper, put their name at the top, and attempt the assignment; do not read books on their reading level and push themselves.

We have our commonalities, Weiss and I.

The void between Abel on one end and the nonreaders and fake readers on the other is too far to measure, too vast to explain.

The beginning of the year is full of hope and potential. Where are my pookies going? How far can I push them? Where will they be in 180 days?

But with the end quickly approaching, there are so many I-should-haves and could-haves, I could fill a room of why-didn't-I's, and I'm feeling particularly angsty and angry about it, but before I can call up Abel, one of my slackers comes up and says, "Ms., why do I have an F in here?"

"You haven't read your last-quarter book," I say to the boy who has annoyed me all year with the contrast between his ability and his effort.

"But I did. I finished that one a long time ago," he says.

"You finished your last book two weeks into this final quarter. I'm not counting that as your last-quarter book."

"But why? I finished it this quarter."

This boy is a lot like Jesus, both cut from the same low-lying tree, the lowest limb, easy to reach with no desire to move upward. Joseph, in particular, has no need for reading, even less so than Jesus last year when I had him in class.

I try to explain a lot of things to him, none of which he understands.

"Books are more than just words to be counted," I say.

"Books are gateways."

Books are the way up and the way out.

Scratch that. Books are only the way out if you happen to know you are in a hole.

Joseph does not.

He thinks he's on the top of the world and books are beneath him.

"Nobody but you is reading for points, Joseph. You're the only one."

I look around the room, correct in my assessment. The only students worthy of discussing this with have outread Joseph, and they had to work harder to read than he has. His test scores are so good he wasn't even supposed to be in this class.

"Go away," I say to Joseph. "You don't understand me, you may never understand me, and you can go finish a freaking baby book if you want just to get your points."

Then, just as quickly, I say, "I changed my mind—I don't care if you flunk; you can read a big book for a big boy or you can just get an F—explain that to your mom."

His mom had written, of course.

Moms.

Imagine if you will a Saturn-sized momma with her baby all swaddled up safe and sound next to her Himalayan-sized bosom, nothing to interfere with his trajectory. No teacher coming in here telling her snookums he needs to read, do work, learn, try.

Her Mercury-sized hand swatting away any teachers who do not comfort and coddle her little moon-boy with his moon-face, one of Saturn's new moons newly discovered … scientists call it *Chipilon*.

I digress.

I send him away and call Abel over. "Bring your book," I add.

In the three-foot walk from his desk to mine, I am struck by the difference of the two distinctly different boys. Gone is the unicorn boy, the winding roots of apathy wrapped around his legs now seemingly severed.

There is a stride to his three short steps and a structure to his form when he sits. He's not quite a king, but he is no pawn either.

"What are you doing to that book? Let me see. When did I give it to you?" I say.

"I don't know. Remember? I had just finished *Chain Reaction* and you said to read this, but I'm reading *Homeboyz* right now too."

Abel leans over my desk on his elbow, our faces almost the

same height. He doesn't come near me like a sixth grader or a huggy kind of kid, always seeking high fives and knuckle bumps. He doesn't seek me out to talk about this or that or tell me about his weekend, but when we do talk, he makes us equal somehow. He leans in, leans over, his face not so far and not so close.

Mathematically this doesn't make sense. He read seven books with a similar number of pages in less time. I'm not sure how he's reading what he's reading, but I know one thing: I was completely wrong.

He's not reading *Always Running* like a blues ballad; it's slower and more methodical, like a dirge or a death march.

I look up at Abel's face and wonder what happened to the boy with the unicorn book, and then I look down and see his latest pencil outline.

It's just a random pink-colored pencil he's using. He doesn't even bother with number-two lead. He's made tiny marks around three words. "I feel trapped."

I flip back through the book. There are multiple marks, many places where he's outlined words and lines.

"Every sentence he writes is like poetry," Abel says. "The book speaks to me."

I look up from the pencil markings.

Are those sideburns?

Is that peach fuzz?

Who is this?

"I liked it too, but I didn't do this," I say as I point now to his markings.

Abel looks down. "Yeah," he says. "Sorry about your book."

A teacher's heart is a delicate thing, tiny pieces allotted for so many kids over so many years. People ask me how I can possibly retire, but this is why. I cannot do this forever. Abel just took a giant chunk, and it is too much for a heart to take.

"You know your name is probably coming up in today's retention meeting, right? There are a few teachers who are still frustrated by your lack of effort and probably want you to repeat eighth grade."

He nods his head.

"You've got to pass that science class, or they're going to make it happen."

"Yeah, I know," he says. "It's just his Newton's law project. I'll get it done. I promise."

With Manny I was holding out on that handshake.

The picture of that ragamuffin kid still in my head, looking around the room, I see now Manny was in survival mode.

As soon as he finished *It Calls You Back*, I was going to put my hand out. He'd put his out, his would be limp and awkward, and I'd say, "No, no, like this," and then I'd hold his wrist with my left hand and gently move his open right hand toward mine until the webs between our thumbs and forefingers met, and then gently I'd wrap my fingers around his hand, and he'd do the same.

With our hands embraced, my grip conveying what my words could not, I'd tell him what I wanted him to know.

I'd say it too, of course, look him in the eye and tell him, "I'm proud of you, Manny."

In my head there was a ticker-tape parade, confetti, streamers, and the Times Square New Year's Eve ball dropped.

Or was that for me? The end of my career just days away, no ticker tape in my future, nothing but a coffee cup that says, "I Used to Teach; Now I Pee When I Want."

I don't tell Maggie about Abel. I can't; there's no way to

explain highlighting and the retention. I couldn't handle it if she didn't understand, and anyway, Celina just strolled by hand in hand with her boyfriend.

"Geezus," I say.

"What?" says Maggie.

"Oh, it's just—I'm not surprised," I nod my head toward Bonnie and Clyde.

She catches my look, follows my eyes. "Oh, the new girl?" she says. "Did you hear?"

"It could be anything," I say, looking down the hallway, seeing Abel and his girlfriend not looking too love birdy. He's trying to get by; she's trying to hold him back. I look again at Maggie, trying to have a normal conversation in an insane asylum a half hour after everyone's meds wore off. "What happened?"

"The new girl told Pacheco he could suck it."

"You've got to be kidding," I say.

"Nope, I think this one is really true because then I heard she crotch-chopped him."

"Is it weird she may be my new hero?"

"Not weird," says Maggie, "but let's see how long that lasts."

"Wish me luck," I say. "She may make it to class today."

I walk into my room, closing the door behind me. The bell has already rung, but I know Celina and Jesus weren't heading to class. I need to prepare myself mentally for the moment Celina arrives, if she arrives.

I take a deep breath, let it out hard, and walk into a talkative bunch, most of whom I have to tell to get out their books. "You only have a couple weeks to finish your final book, people, so get them out."

Teachers need their own version of open/closed signs. On one side it would say how much I loved them all, enjoyed teaching, couldn't wait to change the world.

It would depend on my mood, of course, because the other side would be for the dark times, the times I argued with colleagues and with mean girls.

Days like today there would have to be a third sign, brought out when I'm straining with the weight of the barbell, four hundred pounds of plates on either side, trying to attempt my final clean and jerk. It can be rough on the kid who isn't on his A game because the other side of the sign would be a warning: Slackers Beware.

God help the child who thinks right now is the time to ask to be able to do last night's homework or go to the bathroom like he does every day or go see the nurse because he has a booboo so small there isn't a Band-Aid made to fit or to go see the counselor because something dramatic happened last month or happened last night or is about to happen … These are just some of my thoughts ten minutes into silent reading when the door opens and Celina slinks through.

Tardy is within a minute or two. Ten minutes, on the other hand, is I've-got-more-important-things-going-on-than-this-class.

I take attendance again to mark Celina tardy instead of absent, then I check my email to calm down, give me time to count to one thousand, but I get riled up instead because apparently Weiss found out Manny was gone and decided to move Abel up the retention-notification ladder.

It's no coincidence. Round two of Ms. Russell versus Celina starts right now, Stephen King's *Carrie* is just another teenage angst movie, right?

I need a facade that stays casual while inside every ounce of my being is in fight mode. I have a need to convey that I'm not interested in Celina's antics while being completely unwilling to put up with Celina's antics, a triage nurse who doesn't flinch at the severed leg, doesn't turn away from the gaping chest wound, won't back down when the gang member enters the hospital room to finish the job.

"Come here," I say to Celina.

It surprises her. She's used to getting her way, walking on by, her armor impenetrable. I take a cut anyway.

"Have a seat.

"You've been enrolled here for a while, yet I've only seen you a few times because you ditched my class for days, and when you have come, you seem to always be late. Like today."

"You don't know—"

"Don't do it again," I say.

It's simple, it's quick, and it's to the point. I consider continuing my lecture series, listing the litany of consequences she could encounter, but there are no consequences I can impart on a girl with half a schedule.

I send her back to her seat and keep my vigil from days ago, watching without watching, hounding without interaction, and Celina twiddles her thumbs.

Literally.

I'm grateful group-home kids don't have phones.

"You could write me that personal essay you don't plan on writing or grabbing a book you don't plan on reading," I say, my chances for Teacher of the Year dwindling.

A student gets up and moves to the seat in front of Celina.

"Ariella, move back to your seat."

However, there aren't assigned seats in this class, so the power struggle ensues, my orbit and Celina's orbit pulling Ariella from opposite directions.

There's a twitter in the air. It's hard to describe, but there's whispering without a source, movement without anything moving, tapping, twitching, irritability, and it's not just me and Celina.

Now Angelino is up moving toward Celina.

"Angelino, back to your seat," I say, deadpan, flat, leaving no room for interpretation.

He makes a racket on the way back. Words I've never heard from Angelino. "Why, Ms.? Why you in such a bad mood? What if I don't feel like moving?"

Imagine a rock flying through the window, a bang at the door at midnight, a shotgun blast at an archery range.

Back talk is like that.

"Angelino, Ariella, outside," I say.

I get up, and they get up, but they're grumbling something incomprehensible, gibberish in this classroom where nothing bad has ever happened.

Once we're outside it's as though I'm talking to strangers.

"What are you doing?" I say. "This girl could be gone tomorrow and never come back, and you're just going to do what you want? Say whatever you feel? You never acted like this before she got here."

Everything I feared is happening. I'm losing them both, and I'm not sure how to get them back. They mouth off. I threaten. They mouth off. I say, "Think, really think. She may not even be back tomorrow."

As I walk back into the room, two boys walk up to me and hand me a paper. "This is the note they've been passing with the new girl."

I pull the folded paper apart and remember instantly why I hate opening notes. "Ms. needs a dick up in her. She's one troll-ass bitch. Yeah, she an ugly skank that needs a good fuck."

I call for a monitor and send him with the note and the referral. I send an email too, follow-up to establish my expectations for what will happen next, but if she's at school after telling Pacheco to suck anything, then this little classroom scuffle won't even make the admin radar.

I don't go out for my four minutes of passing period. I'd like to go home, call in sick, take a leave of absence for the next four hours, slip out of the class and into a nice booth in a bar where everyone is twenty-one years old and older, but we don't get to just leave.

A few years back, at the high school down the street, two cheerleaders walked into a classroom and attacked a girl. A teacher got into the middle of the melee, got hit and knocked down, a ten-foot wave crashed in the middle of his classroom.

However, unlike a real wave where the victim drags himself to shore, lays in the sand and recovers, we have to point to the objective on the board, pass out papers and continue with our day.

I check my email over and over again approximately every forty-five seconds after I press "send" to the administration. It's silly actually—I know they aren't writing back; Pacheco wouldn't do anything anyway.

And there's more on my mind.

Abel.

I don't believe in retention, but I believe in consequences.

As my last period of the day begins to settle, get out their books, and start to read, I look down at Manny's book again.

I have so many feelings in this moment, but mostly I feel like I'm cleaning dried flowers on a child-sized grave.

I open to the page with his bookmark, 296, 40 pages left to read, 40 pages to the fucking handshake I should have already given.

Sometimes I really piss me off.

But there are no free hugs and no free handshakes, no butterfly kisses in MUSD.

I refuse to contribute to a handout society. My kids must work for what they get, what I give.

Fucking handshake. That's what I give, nothing but the web of my hand next to his, and it didn't even happen.

Where does that get us?

I want another chance with Manny, and it's never going to happen.

18

CENSOR THIS

Teaching middle school with the finish line in sight is like playing quarterback in the Super Bowl with galoshes on your feet and a gorilla on your back while selling forty-four-ounce beers in the stands while cleaning up the bleachers during the game while moping Bourbon Street during Mardi Gras at midnight.

At the same time.

While riding a merry-go-round.

I dress quickly, only slightly hindered by the love of Sunday's freshly washed sheets and the dread of a Monday workday, the pull of morning Maggie banter enough to get me through the front door, to my room, and back out again for the first passing period.

"Did I tell you I started menopause?" I tell Maggie.

"You don't remember telling me?" she says.

"Did I? Well, I was just thinking, there's no difference."

"Between?"

It's the hallway, it's passing period. Some kids came back from Disneyland Sunday morning, some just went on a STEM overnight fieldtrip, some still haven't figured out how to do school, while others are ready to move on to the next grade.

Sixth graders acting like seventh graders, eighth graders acting like high school kids... chocolate cake with chocolate frosting with chocolate syrup with chocolate sprinkles, all washed down with a chocolate shake.

I work in transitions.

But I don't have to explain all that to Maggie.

"Between menopause and the end of school," I say.

"Ah," she says. "Now I understand menopause."

I look back and forth from one end of the hallway to the next. I want to tell Maggie my dream, but a middle school hallway is no place for that kind of intimacy.

It's day 172, the school day already moving like a tornado backtracking, the apocalypse round two.

First period starts, and Donny is still taking twenty minutes to sharpen a pencil.

Yuliana still has to be personally invited to take out her book.

Andrew still looks at me, looks away, looks at me, looks away. "I'm one hot teacher, aren't I, Andrew?" I say as I brush back my long, gray hair. "I'm hot. I know it. Don't be ashamed to stare."

The class laughs. Andrew looks away and then back at me, away and then back.

His concentration level has not changed since day one.

I'm a failure.

Jason hasn't read one single book, and I still don't know why, his IQ possibly too low, his ability practically nonexistent, yet still they didn't try to retain him.

My only guess is he didn't piss off Weiss or the linebacker or some other teacher obsessed with compliance and hell-bent on revenge.

Annette though—Annette has decided for some unknown reason that she deserves more. She finished *Are You There, God?*

It's Me, Margaret, and she wants *Tiger Eyes* over the summer. I have to buy *Tiger Eyes* before the summer.

It's almost summer.

I wish I got paid more.

And then there was Payton and now just an empty chair. Oh, Payton, with her hand-drawn pen tattoos, her emo hair hanging over her brow and her brain, her monstrous brain being used to learn how to steal from the mall instead of write an essay. Oh, Payton, I'm glad your mom kept you home. These kids are a bad influence. You're the good one, really you are.

It's only nine fifteen.

I wonder if el jefe read my memo about the Xanax machine.

Through the tiny window of my classroom door, I can see Mr. Scott's face. He's beckoning me into the hallway.

"Ms. Russell," says the counselor, "Celina is having a change of plans—there's been some drama at the home where she lives, and she's trying to work through that, but she wants to change, wants to work."

I haven't seen Celina in days.

My only solace is that she spent some time with Mark the Magnificent.

On the way into school, he caught me in the breezeway and said Pacheco didn't want to deal with Celina again, so he put her with the only person with skin thick enough to handle her molten tongue.

He told her, "You must like Mission Heights."

"I fucking hate it here," she said.

"Well, that's a lie. You obviously don't because you're doing everything you can to stay another year."

That made me laugh, but I'm not sure if it was his words or his freaking smirk thinking he's so funny. It also helps knowing my friend got in one good jab before she was sent back to me.

The counselor looks at Celina. "Ms. Russell is a good teacher; she'll give you a chance—"

I stop Mr. Scott before he finishes. "You owe me an apology," I say, looking directly at Celina.

She looks away. "I didn't write it," she says.

"I didn't ask you if you wrote it." I'm clear, not angry, straightforward.

Now that I have a chance with her, I'm going to take it. After this is over, she'll have one teacher, for sure, who didn't dismiss her, who took her seriously, who didn't take shit from her but also didn't give it back.

"I didn't do it," she says again.

I wave my hand toward my door, my students just on the other side. "They've all said they're sorry, every single one of them, sometimes every day, a cuss word here, a rude comment there, but they say they're sorry and we move on, we just—"

She cuts me off. "I'm sorry," she says.

"So," I say, turning to Mr. Scott, "when is she coming back? Right now?"

"No, she's going to spend one more day with Mark and get some of her work caught up."

"Okay." I turn back to Celina. "I'll bring you a book to read, but I'm not fooling around anymore. You're going to read what I give you, even if it kills me."

She turns to Mr. Scott; thoughts pass between them.

They both turn back to me. "She thinks you hate her," he says.

I look at Celina.

"You apologized, and what did I do?"

"You talked about a book."

I ask them both to wait as I walk back into my room and grab *Shattered* off my shelf. I walk back out and place it in Celina's hands.

"Here," I say. "Try this, and I'll come check on you after this class."

She holds the book in her hand, a girl on the cover, her life clearly in ruin. I'm not sure if Celina will even read the first page, but if I were betting, I'd bet not.

Five seconds later, and I'm certain she won't read it.

I walk back into my room and try to turn my attention back to the people in 111, but my mind keeps wandering back to Celina.

If she's legitimately worried about how I feel, then the next time I see her matters more than just now with Mr. Scott.

As soon as the next class ends, I slip into Mark's room, give him a head nod, and walk over to Celina.

It's been an hour since Celina apologized. We're not exactly friends, but we also aren't as we were.

When I pull up a chair next to her, she doesn't even pretend to care about *Shattered*, no interest in finding out what's inside, no desire to impress me by reading a page or two.

"Not your thing?" I say as I pick up the book in front of her.

"I guess not," she says. She's edgy now. Something must have happened.

I look toward Mark.

"The group home isn't too happy with our little friend here," he says.

This makes sense. She lost control, and now someone else has control over her. A kid in her situation needs to misbehave in order to gain control, and the cycle continues.

I place a copy of *Perfect Chemistry* in front of her.

"I know you don't read—don't worry; no one reads when they come to my class." I tap the cover. "But I think you'll like this."

She flips it over and reads the back.

I can see by the movement of her eyes that the connection is being made. This book is like that, tasty teen drama I wouldn't read for a hundred dollars.

"This is my girls' favorite book," I say. Teens in general, the one commonality she has with a kid who lives in a home with her own family, parents with real jobs, kids who vacation during Christmas break and camp during summer break.

She's weary, like Manny, so many in their past that crossed them, too many words unknown, too many strings attached, adult approval, worksheets, dioramas, and book reports.

For the last hour, I've been obsessing over what I'd say with my one chance with the girl who may not be back tomorrow or the next day or the next.

"The thing is, I don't know anything about you, but I know where you live, and books are one thing you can control. The book will be yours—your feelings, your thoughts—and once you've finished the book, no one can take it away from you."

She looks down at her shoe, reaches down, and brushes off a speck of dust only Celina can see.

"You need to know someone will always have it worse than you—not only you but other girls in that group home."

Now she looks at me.

Other girls.

"If you read this, then you can give it to someone else at the home and then there are two of you with something no one else can take away."

I try to picture just how many adults have been through this child's life, how many have violated her trust, her youth, her innocence. I refuse to be categorized with them.

"If I'm wrong then you can do whatever you want with the book." I pause, look at her closer. I can see now the lipstick, the eyeliner, the mascara, they're all part of the warrior facade. "Books will change your life; just trust me."

I pat her on the knee too.

"You can do this."

"All right. I'll try," she says.

It's not her words but a look she gives me. I tell her I'll drop by Mark's to see where she is, how much she's read.

But this time I wait. We talk about making connections. I sit as she reads the first page. I need to make sure the fluid starts to flow, no kink in the line preventing the patient from receiving her inoculation.

~

If there were a Xanax machine in the teacher's lounge, it would be just like all the other vending machines at the end of the school year, void of teaching staples, empty of sugary vestibules fueling our tired bodies, the last Snickers bar stuck at the back of the rack, holding on for dear life.

The Xanax dispenser no different, deprived teacher hands grasping the sides of the glass enclosure and shaking, tipping back and forth, trying to get the last magical oval-shaped oh-look-my-house-is-burning-but-I-don't-care on the last row to drop.

Back in the hallway, Maggie tells me about the tube of anal lubricant she found on the floor.

I tell her about the kids who were paper arrested while on a field trip at Ed's place across the street.

She says she found a condom in the recycle bin.

I say, "I heard Rodriguez asked a kid to sweep behind the bookshelf, and there was a dead mouse."

She says, "I heard—" but then Mark walks up, and their words overlap.

He says, "Did you hear about the fight in the sixth-grade hall?"
And then Maggie says, "Well, did you hear about the sub in Weiss's room?"

We're loud at this point, laughing like a group of people more likely with pretzels and beers in their hands than chalk and glue sticks.

Someone else walks up and leans in, and we know something good is coming our way. We lean in too, closer, tighter. We want to know what happened.

What happened?

Tell us what happened.

Then she whispers low. "Did you hear about Huicochea's room?"

We set our beers down because now we're hoping for a sex scandal, a holy-shit, she's-so-messed-up kind of belly laugh. Huicochea is a teacher with questionable teaching skills with a classroom full of students with intellectual disabilities.

This is going to be so, so good.

What? What? What? We say with our bodies, our eyes, and our ears.

She looks around her circle of groupies. She knows she has us hanging on, waiting for the latest and greatest scandal of the year.

I look around too. Maybe it's to feel better about my twenty-nine years of mistakes, maybe just to remember teachers are not only human but we are fallible too—in my case, egregiously fallible.

Then slowly our colleague's words come out. She wants to make sure we can see the picture clearly, visualize what she's been visualizing until she could tell us, until she could share the load she's been carrying. "She had one of her female students taking one of her male students to the bathroom."

Someone says, "What?"

But no one really wants it repeated; no one wants to hear again something they cannot unhear the first time.

"What?" someone else says.

"She has been rewarding a girl for her behavior by having her take a boy—who needs extra help—to the bathroom."

Choices.

Some better than others.

The winner of the One-Up Club has just dropped the chalk.

We walk away, our beers left half empty on the table behind us. We have to get back; our students need us.

Statistically speaking students may begin showing signs of eighth-grade-itis as early as September or October. Regardless of the onset and speed with which the disease may spread, there will be a full-on epidemic with three weeks left of school.

Seven days?

Everyone is infected, and the side effects are devastating to those of us still attempting to squeeze knowledge into what was once vacuous but is now filled with summer dreams and pre–high school tittering. Keeping the desks in line, sweeping Takis off the floor, and catching paper planes as they fly past by our periphery is about all some of us can do.

Roller coasters are for the weak.

"Get your books out, people," I say as I head toward my desk to take attendance and think about these next days wrapping up without checking out.

Even the best of kids need reminders that mothers and fathers who are at work expect their babies to be working at school.

I took inspirational steps toward leading my little horsies to drink by putting in one hundred points for the final book check.

No book, no points.

No points equals a big, bold F right there on a final report card, a last statement to mommies and daddies as little pookie begins to make public-pool swim plans with his friends, trips to the movies and the skate park, and sleepovers all at risk on the F slide.

A week ago I took a piece of chalk to the blackboard and sent a message. "Your final book check is due by May 23rd. It is worth 100 points. If you do not finish your final book, there is about a 100 percent chance you will have an F for the quarter."

I signed it sweetly and sincerely, "Ms. Russell," drew hearts around it.

I put one hundred points possible in the grade book, and then I gave everyone 100 or 0.

The kids whose moms are chronic grade checkers ask if there is an alternative to the book assignment. "Like a worksheet or something?"

"Um, no."

The only replacement for reading a book is reading a book.

And I'll be specific. Here are some end-of-the-year don'ts and don'ts.

1. Don't say you've read all the pages when you've skipped forty of them. I've been watching you, and I know what you are capable of doing.
2. Don't think saying, "I read it, but I left it at home," will get you one hundred sympathy points.
3. Don't think saying, "I lost it," will get you actual points.
4. Don't blame me or your parents or your life for not reading one book in nine weeks, and if you didn't read it, don't say, "I tried."
5. Don't switch *The Secret Garden* original version for *The Secret Garden* condensed fourth-grade version and say, "I lost the other one, but it's the same."

I look up at Diego before calling him over.

I still remember handing him *Tyrell*, pointing around the room, telling him, "See those guys, there and there?" I kept pointing. "They all read it."

He looked around too. He had to see if the right people read what he was committing to read. "All right," he said.

He finished in a month, almost every day the same. "Diego, get your book out."

"Diego, get your book out."

Every day.

Unless he was absent.

A few weeks later, he walked up and set it down on my desk. "Finished," he said.

"What's the theme?" I said.

"Someone always has it worse than you?" he said. "Never give up?" he added, his sentences questions rather than statements.

I admitted I hadn't read it.

"What? You haven't read *Tyrell*? It's good, Ms. You should read it."

I laughed. "No, thanks. I don't like to read about teen sex."

He laughed too. "I get you," he said. "Well, I think *Tyrell* is about overcoming stuff—because he realizes what his dad is like, and he doesn't want to be like him—same for his mom."

I wanted to ask him if that's what his mom and dad were like, but I didn't.

Today, though, with *Bronxwood*, I call him to my desk and ask him what I want to know. "What can you relate to? What parts?" I say.

"In *Bronxwood*?" He flips the book over in his hand. "Eating," he says. Tyrell is always hungry—I'm always hungry." He says it like he's hungry now, like a boy who could eat a pizza by himself.

"Which is weird," he adds. "I give my lunch away every day."

What?

"Every day?" I say.

What? What? What?

"Yeah, there's this girl—Destiny? Do you know her?"

I nod my head.

"Well, one day she says, 'You get free lunch, right? Will you get me lunch?' so I'm like, 'Sure.'" He pauses and looks at me like he could be in trouble for something, breaking a cafeteria rule about sharing free food. "So, I've been giving her my lunch every day."

"You're a jerk," I say.

"What? Why? What'd I do?" he says, not knowing what I mean, but knowing I am teasing him, finally being able to tease him. He smiles. "What?"

"I swear I was going to kill you almost every day of school— getting you to read *Tyrell* almost killed me—and now I'm calling you over just to talk about *Bronxwood*, and now I just want to cry."

"Why Ms.? Why?"

"Let me see your book," I say.

He slides *Bronxwood* over to me. I don't have many copies of this book, but I've had at least a hundred guys and a handful of girls read it. It's also the book most stolen.

MUSD librarians got together and decided *Tyrell* was a high school book. Luckily I don't use the library. Censorship is such a confusing and controversial concept.

I pull out my drawer and reach for a pen.

"What are you doing, Ms.?"

"Whatever I want."

We've made it to day 173, and Diego made it for almost 90 of them, if nothing else happens between now and May 23.

I open the book to the first page that looks blank enough for me to write on.

"Ms., you can't give me that book," he says, like I'm the one breaking rules now instead of the food-giver.

"Yeah, I can Diego—welcome to public school," I say.

I write the date and his name, and then I write what I want to say.

It's the lunch that did it.

Diego saw someone worse off than himself, and he reached out.

"You're going to be all right, Diego," I say, still looking down as I write, holding back a tear I don't feel like showing.

"Really?" he says.

I look up. "You know why I wrote that hoodie thing on the board?"

I want to make sure he hears me, if my freaking tear betrays me, so be it.

"I wrote that for you, so you wouldn't fight with me. I wanted you to have a chance to succeed, and that wasn't going to happen if we were fighting. You needed me on your team, not against you."

"But other kids got in trouble for that."

He's right. Two completely normal students without oppositional behavior would end up with their hoodies still on after the bell almost every day. In the past I would have said, "Take off your hoodie," but I couldn't risk that with Diego, so the boys had to put their hoodies on my desk. The trade-off was worth it; although, it says something that Diego recognized there were casualties.

"Yep, but you made it through eighth grade."

"Well, I'm not really passing," he says, and he's right, but the eighth-grade team already decided he was moving to high school.

"Why do you say I'll be all right?"

"Because one day you're going to be a man, and a boy is going to come to you and he's going to be just like you and he'll need help and you're going to know exactly how to help him."

"You know that because I got someone food?"

"Yeah, because you got someone some food."

I finish writing in his book and hand it to him. "I know you'll finish this one day, and if not, you can still keep it with you—oh, remember that time with Rodriguez? How she let you wear your sweatshirt? I did that too."

I had to tell him, had to let him know how much trouble one person went to in order to make him successful.

He smiles, and it seems like he has something to say, but my door swings open, and in walks Mark. I don't like the look on his face, so I'm not surprised when he says, "You aren't going to like this."

I pat Diego on his knee and ask him to excuse us.

Mark sits on the stool and leans toward me.

"They have Jesus up in the office with the police—"

"Who else?" I say, but he doesn't have to say the name. I can tell by the look on his face that Abel isn't coming back to school.

I look up at my clock and do the math—the anal lubricant was twenty years ago. I look around the room for my next victim and realize I was wrong about my war on apathy. A child cannot be apathetic. They are far too young to be entrenched in such deep-seated discontent.

Instead I wage my battle upon a child's less-than-personal beliefs, and I help them fight intrinsically because the war is and will always be Man Versus Self.

I heard a lecture series once, a professor at the old college of Ed across the street. He ranted and raved about the "white saviors." He pointed and shouted, called out all the light-skinned people in the room for trying to save the kids, the white parents taking the black kid off the street, the white teacher teaching in the ghetto…all his racism echoing out in Ed's Kiva Auditorium.

I wish, El Professor, but that's not how this goes.

Teachers don't save.

If I could I'd purchase my own helicopter, pick up Abel and Gero and a litany of others. I'd drop them all onto a tall ship with giant sails in the middle of the ocean. They would spend the month sailing around from island to island with a few adults who knew a little about adulting. If they wanted to come back, I'd say, "But are you ready? Can you choose of your own free will, or must you still follow the footsteps of those in your family and those in your neighborhood?" If the answer is no, I'd send them back, no one leaving the ship until the chains to their neighborhoods were so paper thin, even the Jesuses of the world could not tear them.

Does that make me a white savior?

No.

I can't save anyone.

You know what I have?

A book and a handshake.

That's all most of us have. Just a bunch of people seeing tragedy and deciding what to do about that tragedy, and sometimes it looks like saving, but most of the time it's just a change of trajectory, our children so entrenched in their orbital path they need something thrown at them to knock them off their course.

I throw books.

Mark throws basketballs.

The science teacher throws Newton's laws.

Rodriguez throws the Constitution and the Bill of Rights and all the amendments, including the ones she believes are abused.

The math teacher throws perseverance and intent, and she demands her children answer on purpose. Eleven-year-olds?

The audacity, que no?

Eleven-year-olds don't do anything on purpose, their lives haphazard, brushing their teeth only done because they were told to brush.

Don't even get me started on what my elementary school teaching compadres throw. Everything. Anything.

I'm so mad.

I don't know why.

Or maybe I do.

I've seen enough daytime talk shows to know mad means afraid, and I am afraid.

I'm afraid Abel hasn't read enough to break the mental poverty that binds him to his roots, and I'm afraid Destiny's mom will kill all of the Destiny I know and the Destiny I love, and I'm afraid Celina will turn out just like her mother and her father.

And what can I do about all of it?

Nothing.

Nothing except knock a few more kids off their fucking trajectory.

∼

It's not until I gather my things to go home that I even notice, chalkboard writing almost always stating I'm someone's favorite teacher or someone is my favorite student.

But this is no juvenile love note.

I leave it up and take a picture for my social media profile. It will pair nicely with my cockroach picture from earlier in the year. Someone managed to sum up my life's work in three words, my epitaph thirty years early, and they put it right next to my name.

Ms. Russell Read or Die.

19

ABEL

"There is nothing noble in being superior to your fellow man.
True nobility is being superior to your former self."
—ERNEST HEMINGWAY

Where I work, a smack on the back of the head is called "neck."

When the principal announces the water will be turned off for this reason or that, someone always raises a hand.

"Yes, Junior?"

"Can I go to the restroom?"

Neck.

Seventh period, kids read silently for twenty minutes, then I pass out papers for kids to take notes on the lesson. When everything is passed out and I'm ready to teach, Junior says (more often than not), "I need a pencil."

Neck.

Kid asks, "Is ham pig?

Neck.

"Ms., is that your natural color?"

Neck.

"Ms., are you married?"

Neck. Neck.

Slapping a kid in the back of the head, barbaric, I know, but it's May.

One student's brain is firing like a pinball arcade, but her auditory-to-brain messages are lightning strikes over arid land. "I don't get you," she says, her face twisted sideways.

We're the crazy ones, not her.

I say, "Neck," but I don't really mean it.

"Neck!" someone yells.

"Neck," someone echoes.

Someone always offers, but I never accept. I can't help but act like I'm all in favor of the necking this kid is about to get, but in the end I say, "No, Abel, you can't smack Gero on the back of the head. I'd have to write you up."

I laugh, of course, and ask if anyone would tell on me if I hid certain student bodies under the school...

I wasn't lying about not being Teacher of the Year material.

For almost two years our school has been handing out teacher-of-the-month awards. It was Pacheco's idea. At some point he decided drawing names from a coffee can was not a way to pick a recipient for such a prestigious award.

With the new award, the recipient gets prime parking plus a painted porcelain Bulldog to poise on their desk. I heard the dog was broken once and glued back together, but I wouldn't know. The only time I was teacher of the month was when my name was drawn out of the coffee can.

At our passing-period stations, Maggie says, "I had a kid walk in fifteen minutes late, high as a kite. I asked her for a pass, but I don't think she had any idea what I was saying."

Mark walks up and says, "At the end of the year, I write on the chalkboard: If you're going to be stupid, be stupid at home, not at school."

"She was too stoned to hide the bag, so she was paper arrested," Maggie says.

I won't miss PD, but I sure will miss meetings of the OUC.

"I heard the sixth-grade team just had their entire collection of field trip money stolen by some new kid—handed it out at lunch and told everyone his dad was in the Mexican Mafia."

"There's an eighth grader spraying disinfectant in everyone's mouth."

A kid prank-called Salazar's room from the room next door and said there was a bomb threat.

A kid brought a knife.

There were three fights at lunch.

I heard Pacheco wouldn't deal with disinfectant girl.

"But we have to teach with all the disinfectant kids in class," one of us says.

"Exactly," one of us says.

"Exactly," someone else says.

Somewhere between the knife and the disinfectant, I suddenly remember Maria's homework assignment.

I call her over and ask her how it went.

"Did you do it?" I say.

"I did," she says. "I knew you were right when he started crying—who cries over a middle school breakup? It's middle school. Seriously."

She's older than last time we talked.

How did that happen?

She asks me what I'm going to do in retirement. "Aren't you going to miss helping kids?"

We never did fix the "weirdo" comment.

Or maybe we did.

"I have to figure out a way to get books to kids," I say.

"Why don't you get a van?" she says. "You can put 'read or die' on the side and drive around town."

"You saw that, did you? I still don't know who wrote it— wait. A van? That's a great idea."

My teacher fantasies suddenly filled with a van and an ice cream facade. No Bomb Pops or ice cream sandwiches in this automotive masterpiece, just books written by authors who want to change children's trajectories.

"I'll play 'Pop Goes the Weasel' on repeat," I say, "and dress like a creepy clown."

Later when I have forty-five seconds to spare, I hustle to the workroom to check my box for messages about Abel.

Of course Weiss is there. "I heard we make fifteen hundred subconscious decisions a day," she says, her pinky turned upward with her teacup handle as she orates to one of her disciples. "I don't think that's true. I am completely aware of every decision I make."

I love the bartenders who give drinks *on the house.*

It's just another way of saying, "Let's keep this between us."

Nothing like a free drink to loosen my pockets and free up my change.

When you're under a forty-year-old court order, you pad your numbers and tell parents to keep kids home instead of doing all the paperwork to document the suspension.

"Let's just keep it between us," administrators say, sincerely of course; they don't want this getting out either.

Typically for out-of-school suspensions, we get a paper in our mailbox, but there's still nothing on Abel, and my best informant remains my fourteen-year-old, Gero.

"I don't know, Ms. I'm not stupid. Jesus told me to go in there with him, and I'm like, 'Heck no,'" he says. "My mom took away my phone, and I want it back."

I'm thinking maybe I can give Gero's mom Mrs. Henderson's number, and they can go shopping together…possibly stopping by Shoes R Us and picking up a new pair of chanklas for Mrs. Henderson. They could go out target practicing afterward, coffee in one hand, chankla in the other, a cardboard cutout of little Henderson to work on their aim.

Between classes I stop by Mark's to use the bathroom. When I get there, I am prepared to see Celina in her usual anti-dress-code attire, but I'm not prepared for her face.

"I'm on page 193," she says.

Everything else is the same, the heavy eyeliner, heavier lipstick, and overplucked eyebrows, but now there's a contrast, her lips pulled back in a way I thought impossible for this girl.

I'm in awe.

I thought this baby had forgotten how to smile, five or six foster homes ago the last time those eyes had scrunched together and sparkled.

"You sure are happy," I say.

"I'm usually not a smiley person," she says, "but this is just so good."

She accentuates the "good" like it's the best thing she's ever eaten, a mouthwatering savory dinner with a decadent dessert on the side. Move over and let me at that pie.

"You're on page 193?" I say. Holy crap, I don't say.

I was only heading through Mark's to the adult bathroom. Having Celina halfway through her book is a teacher's heart attack waiting to happen.

That she came to school out of uniform?

Yes.

That she read even one page of *Perfect Chemistry*?

No.

"Yeah, but I didn't bring it with me," she says.

Now this makes sense.

I would ask her what has happened so far if I'd read it. I would consider asking a classmate to quiz her, but here in Mark's room, no one can confirm or deny what Celina just said.

What do I say?

What could I possibly say to the girl who may or may not be reading, who may or may not run away from the group home any minute, who I may or may not see again after this moment, who may or may not be placed back with the woman who lost her to the system in the first place, a child who has probably seen more violence and drug abuse in real life than I've seen on television, who has been angry, neglected, and confused most likely her entire life?

My triage training helps; my time with Ed does not.

"Oh," I say, my teaching brain working in slow-mo, biding time for more words, my words that must be carefully crafted because there's no time for misunderstanding.

Celina.

In the beginning my students don't even fake read without being told, but after my class, after a book is in their hands, they can no longer resist, and something happens, something changes; they take their books home and read on purpose. Their own personal purpose. I do not assign reading as homework. I just hope my students read at home, I pray, I cross all my fingers and all my toes, but I do not assign reading as homework.

Then comes the day they get caught.

"She thinks you're on drugs, doesn't she?"

"Yes!" the child will say, and then we'll laugh because we know something, a secret something that no one else knows.

And then we'll retell the story and the class will laugh and someone will say, "No way!" and someone else will say, "That happened to me!" and then we laugh more.

It's a fun time.

But that's never going to happen. Celina doesn't have an adult to catch her reading.

I think of two or three more ideas, more connections, more triage on top of triage, and then I remember our last conversation and I remember sometimes it's easy to be a teacher because sometimes I don't really have to work so hard.

"Any of the girls at the home see you reading?" I say.

She smiles again. "Yes," she says.

"A girl?"

She nods her head.

"She see the cover?"

She nods her head, two teenagers making out on the cover—a great enticement to wonder what's inside, seduction an important aspect of narration.

"Think she'll read it when you finish?"

"I think so," she says.

"Cool," I say, relieved I didn't accuse her of not reading nor give her false compliments I wasn't sure she deserved. "If I don't see you again, just keep it and let the other girl read it when you finish."

The bell rings, of course, and I don't get to pee.

I pat Celina on the shoulder as I leave. "Nice job," I say. I can't help it. I have to compliment her. Dammit, I hope she read.

I head back to class. When I get there, half of them are inside; half are out. Half abiding by the school rules, the other half abiding to rules of nature involving socialization, getting in their last hugs, high fives, and what-are-you-doing-after-school conversations before being corralled into our classroom spaces for another hour.

The socializers see me walking toward the door, and someone says, "I thought we had a sub," relieved I'm still there, knowing the last Friday of the year is more chaotic if the regular adults don't show. What the kids don't know is our principal already told us not to take any more days off work. No substitutes to be found at times like these.

Someone else says, "I thought we had a sub," like he wished he had, but then he smirks at me in that way only someone who cares about you can smirk.

The closer I get to the door, the more I'm a bouncer at a nightclub. I push and shove them into the room, starting with the smirker. He exaggerates my push, falls backward, and yells, "Help! Get me a monitor."

"I'll get you a monitor," I say, "to take you to the nurse."

"Did you guys hear that? Did you hear that? She threatened me," he cries, and we laugh like two old friends who have been through war together. Teachers and students do go through war together, if we're lucky.

When my fourth period starts, two members of our downtown office slip in stealthily, ninjas with comb-overs and short-sleeved dress shirts, graying roots and pantsuits, badges and clipboards.

The district loves themselves some observations. The superintendent from my childhood penned an entire pedagogy, *Mastering the Three-Minute Walk-Through*, deputizing thousands of educational gurus into categorizing teachers, no one telling him teachers are not musical notes. A game show contestant cannot "name that teacher" in three minutes.

They do it anyway.

"Watch out for the woman," Maggie told me before school began. "She doesn't believe in fours."

"Job security," I said. Midlife career changers unprepared for the corporate world, unable to handle the rigor of keeping thirty kids occupied, yet also unprepared to become full-fledged administrators, become evaluators, professional check markers, mathematicians measuring the immeasurable.

They come into my home, no introduction, not even a head nod, just an awkward smile and a mutual understanding. *You know why we're here. Don't mind us.*

When I turn to address the room, a full three minutes into what should have been silent reading, someone says, "Aw, Ms. Do we have to read today?"

Someone else says, "Dude, we have four days of school—Ms. isn't going to change now."

Then someone points to the chalkboard. "Read or die, dude."

I smile and then remember the district representative scribbling away on her little clipboard, no idea what just happened, probably no idea I have four more days of more than half a lifetime in a room with children.

I sigh.

She's looking for an objective, something that will tell her what we're doing. She wants words like, "Students will be able to identify the theme," and, "Students will compare the motivations of two characters," and, "Students will be able to paraphrase the text..."

I kick myself.

I should have clarified.

May 22, 2018
Objective: Students will read or die.

I sigh again.

Like the bubble counters, these people are all about the output. While they look around for evidence to support my average teaching ability, I fantasize about a classroom with electrodes and monitors so I can see the goings on inside my students' heads— no need for pencil and paper in my room, unless of course I'm grading on output, which I do, but not right now.

On paper I imagine I'm the worst teacher on the planet, and the proximity of these two isn't going to help my score. Neither of them are close enough to hear my conversations with my students.

I call over my blue-haired sweetie anyway.

"Hey," I say.

"Hey," she says.

"It's been quite a year, hasn't it?" I say "quite a year," but I mean "Your mom got you back and she doesn't deserve you, and you pretty much outread the school this year," but I don't say either of those.

"What book was your favorite?" I say as I point to the book she brought me, her bookmark sticking out with about a hundred pages remaining of a six-hundred-page book.

"The third one," she says.

"Of that series?" I say, not really understanding what she read, her book palate much different than my own, her books full of dragons and magic, mine full of people and the decisions we make.

Destiny answers my questions and talks on about the year, about the books she liked, the books she didn't, the different books she read, and her infinite questions about what may happen to the dragons and vampires in the books of her future.

I'm listening, of course, but I'm also looking around my room, checking to see if my cherubs are on task while also lamenting the empty desks.

I miss Abel.

His teenage face, his preman body, his colored pencils and delicate fingers marking words that speak to him.

Suddenly a haiku comes to me. These evaluators much more inspirational than I first thought. I want to get on my email, but they would look me up and down, shake their heads, and emphatically scribble their disappointment. It's tragic really. They have no idea the importance of the poem I want to write to Maggie.

I glance out the window instead, Ed's recreation center across the street, college boys and girls buzzing back and forth from their living spaces to the classrooms of higher education, educational futures already within their grasp.

I look back to my room, my cornfield rows of Barrio Sobaco offspring, their futures so tentative, their lives precariously pointing elsewhere, sans interior guides already implanted in those people outside my window.

I hear the door open, and I turn my head.

He walks toward me like everything is fine, like everyone just missed three days of school, like no one was sitting here wondering what happened to him, but Abel's gait is different. The saunter is gone.

He sets a late slip down on my desk. "Can I talk to you?" he says.

Can you talk to me?

Are you kidding?

"Yeah, sure," I say.

I look at him like I'm going to kill him, of course.

"What?" he says from his perch on my stool, playacting like

I'm his mother nagging him about his dirty room and lackluster attempts to help around the house.

"Where have you been?" I say.

"Oh, nowhere, well, Mexico," he says. "My tia needed our help moving—that's it, but all that driving in the car gave me time to finish this."

He sets *Homeboyz* down between us.

"It was so good—oh, I finished *Always Running* too, but I left it at home."

I pick up *Homeboyz*.

This Abel is not so different than the Abel from nine months ago, yet like a crab who has completely molted, leaving behind only a semblance of himself, not himself any longer.

"Oh, and I have my project for science."

Correction.

This isn't Abel at all.

I open his book just to give my hands something to do, to distract me from this moment because it's too much.

"Wait, wait, I want to show you something," he says. He takes the book back; his bookmark falls to the ground. I reach down and pick it up. It's not just a scrap of paper, a placeholder ripped haphazardly. This is a strip of paper, carefully cut. His handwriting covers one side.

Here's friend, here's enemy; here's sadness, here's happiness; here's right, here's wrong.

"That's my favorite quote from *Always Running*," he says. "My dad always said, 'Don't trust anybody.'"

"Is that what this is about?" I point to the bookmark. "Not trusting anyone?"

"I don't think that's what the author meant, but this whole book makes me think of my dad's life—it is his life, back in

Mexico—his cousins—all of it—my dad was never happy." He looks at me. "I don't want to be like that."

I hand him back his paper as he flips through *Homeboyz*. I'm grateful. It gives me time to think, time to recognize I'm completely unprepared for this conversation.

"Check this out." He hands the book back and points to the passage. "This is the main character talking to a police officer. He wants to know how a school can pass his friend along if his friend can't read—see that," he says, his finger demanding my attention to the words. "They use the test results to determine how many jail cells to build," he says.

I keep following his pointing until I get to the paragraph he wants me to see, the one that's fueled this flame inside him.

> Look at the number of fourth grade minority boys reading way below grade level, factor in... poverty... and the percentage of their parents... in prison. Add it all up and you'll have a pretty good indicator of how many jail cells the state is going to need to accommodate all of these kids...

I've been remiss. Pearson obviously cares much more for my students' scores than I thought.

"You know I was almost in trouble, right?" he says.

You mean the picture of the police here and you leaving in handcuffs that I can't get out of my mind? The scene I cannot possibly unsee, even though I don't even know what happened, my teacher imagination occasionally much worse than the truth.

"I heard about it," I say.

"Well, when I was in there with Pacheco and he asked me what happened, I told him I never touched the stuff—I thought Jesus and I were friends, but he tried to pin it all on me. My dad told me they don't build coffins with bunk beds, but this is the first time I understood what he meant."

"Did Pacheco believe you?" I say.

"He did. He said I seemed to be trying to change—I guess it was that application I asked for."

I can still see the unicorn boy—he's somewhere in there—but I also believe he's gone, replaced by this boy, the one who wants more.

"So why this paragraph? Why is this the one that spoke to you?"

"Don't you understand, Ms.?" He sits up straight in this moment, pointing toward *Homeboyz*, a book I've never read and have no interest in reading.

"Don't you get it?" he says. "That could have been me."

Choices.

Abel has choices.

"You know what I do all day?" I say.

"I don't know—teach? Read?" he says, smiles when he says "read."

I laugh. "Yeah, when I'm not teaching you little brats."

"I bet you just sit at home and sharpen your pitchfork," he says.

Now he laughs.

He's not so far off, a drawing from a student framed in my hallway at home, me as the devil at the doorway, my classroom on fire, children screaming for help from the inside, a talking bubble above my head stating the obvious. *"Read!"*

I ask if he knows what an outlier is.

"It's those numbers that don't fit with the other numbers," he says. "We learned that in math."

I explain how outliers work in real life too, that people can be outliers, the first one to graduate from the family, the first one to move out of the neighborhood, the first one to go to college—"The kid who outlines his book."

He points to himself.

I point too.

"You made me realize I not only look for outliers, but I literally try to make outliers out of kids."

Every single kid.

I barely thought it through myself, but that's what I've been doing.

I haven't wanted to teach children how to be sheep or cattle or any other animal that goes with the flow, that lines up in purty little lines, that votes Democrat because their parents vote Democrat.

I've spent my career trying to teach children to reach, to be the ones who question, the ones who can go with the flow when necessary and choose to go against when possible.

Choices.

"Oh, I forgot to ask you," I say. "What happened with that job? Did you get it?"

"I didn't tell you?" he says. "Well, it's not for sure, but it's the one I put in for."

I'm prepared for him to say a painter or a framer or even part of the freeway cleanup crew. I've been here so many times before, same old county jobs for teens, same old story.

And then like he's said it a thousand times, repeated it slowly even more, as matter-of-factly as I say I'm going to get a cup of coffee or have my nails done, Abel tells me what he's going to be doing all summer.

"Working at the library," he says. "That way I can be surrounded by books."

I can't even blame Ed this time.

No one could have prepared me for this.

"The library? Are you serious?"

"Yeah, why? Is that weird?"

"Weird, um, no. It's unbelievable—like actually unbelievable. If I wrote a book about you, no one would believe it."

20

180 DAYS

I don't know when the evaluators left or what they saw or what they said about my class, communication still being MUSD's missing key.

I just know I couldn't sum up the energy to send Maggie my haiku. If I get a chance, I'll send it through the school mail to the visitors, an anonymous gift to those who gave up teaching in order to evaluate those who have not.

Why bother looking
That which is most important
Is immeasurable

The morning sports headlines sit on Mark's desk when I walk into his room.

"They won, didn't they?"

"Yep, five to zero. Not even close."

The Pueblo teams are having a killer year, more so than past years.

"Do you know anyone who works there?"

"The athletic director and the boys' basketball coach," says Mark.

"Ten bucks says they raised the standard on grades."

"No doubt. I know for a fact the girls' basketball players have to have Cs or better to play."

So many letters to write! So little time!

Dear MUSD,

Raise the bar. The students will rise.

Sincerely,
Me

There's no reason to put my name; no one in leadership even knows I exist, and after tomorrow I won't.

It's passing period, I'm in the hallway, and my students are milling around, the urgency of getting places completely erased from their memories, the tardy bell just an inconvenience now.

I'm by my door with Maria. We're watching all the crazies in the hallway when a boy walks up and gets a hug from Maria.

He has enough charisma to get hugs from eighth-grade girls, but from the looks of his baby face, I can only assume he's a sixth grader, his tired shoes and tattered pants plus the multistained shirt says he could be from Barrio Sobaco, if not far from there.

"Hey, what's your name?" I say.

His answer is barely audible. A boy like this is used to strangers accusing him of misbehavior: "What's your name? Why did you do that?"

I ask again, repeating what I think I heard. "Brian?"

"Ryan," he says more clearly.

"Ryan," Maria says.

"Oh," I say. "I've heard of you."

This is not an accusation.

His name has come up frequently in our Kid Talk discussions. He is too old to be retained again and too naughty not to be on our exclusive time-out plan with Mark the Magnificent.

I look at him, judging his success with reading, his success in school based on his body language, facial expression, and level of perceived confidence.

Check boxes.

I never said I didn't have any.

"I'm Ms. Russell," I say. "Nice to meet you."

Slowly, carefully I keep eye contact, my own brand of drug I'm injecting. I'm going to tell the counselor to put you in my room...

Crap.

I'm not coming back next year.

Maria looks at me.

"What?" I say.

"You were going to get him to read a book, weren't you?" she says. "We know you, Ms. You're so predictable—admit it, you're going to miss us."

"I admit to nothing," I say, and I can't. It's still too early to cry.

Down the hallway I see Celina heading our way.

"Celina!" I yell and I laugh and I keep laughing as I walk toward her.

The eighth graders have free-dress, a gift bestowed on them by el jefe in the final three days of school.

I hug her, then hold her at arms' length, look her up and down.

"You're in uniform," I say.

"The head of the group home made me," she says.

I laugh. I have to laugh. This kid just does not get *school*, but she's trying.

"Did the group home head make you bring your book?"

"No, that was my idea," she says.

She holds up *Perfect Chemistry*, and happiness consumes her.

This is my supplemental income.

"You're finished?" I say, but it's just a formality. I know what finishing a first book looks like. Celina has just run her first marathon and won, sans the exhaustion and fatigue that comes with running twenty-six miles. She is elation.

"Come to my stool," I say as we step out of the hallway into my empty room. "I don't know if you were ever here for this, but I sit at my desk, and you sit on the stool."

I point to the inquisition seat as I sit in my chair, swinging around to face Celina.

She's still smiling.

I temper the moment, but I can't honestly say I do it for Celina's sake or to avoid my heart from breaking.

These kids.

They are so beautiful.

"I ask you questions, you answer them perfectly, and then balloons drop from the ceiling and confetti is thrown all over the room."

"Really?" she says.

"No, not really," I say, but I regret saying it. I believe part of her really did think that was true, finishing a book quite a remarkable achievement. "I do ask you questions, though, and then I put in one hundred points for your grade—are you being promoted?"

"No one said I wasn't," she says.

And that's probably true. No one would go to the trouble to retain a student they've barely seen, revenge being such a significant part of retention.

"Well, I'll give you a passing grade for whatever that's worth—reading the book is more important than the points anyway.

"First of all, who died?"

She answers quickly, deftly.

I ask how it ends for Alex.

She answers.

"What about Martin?"

I smile; Celina radiates.

"Dang. You really read it."

"I told you I did."

"First book ever?"

She nods her head, still smiling.

I wish I had confetti and streamers to fall from the ceiling right now. We've come so far in so little time.

What if I'd had 180 days?

"Do you want the next book? I think I have a copy."

She says she does, and I reach into my desk for *Rules of Attraction*, thankful I have a copy someone just returned.

I hold out my hand for *Perfect Chemistry*, but when she places it in my hand, she follows the book with her eyes like a loved one walking away.

Is it possible?

"Do you want to take this back to the home? Do you need this for someone else?"

Celina smiles. She's full of smiles today. "Yes," she says.

Not so different than the thoughts I have before I let Maria go to the bathroom, I have the same number about Celina, only these are like bumper cars at the fairgrounds, ramming into each other over and over again, my head jerking back and forth with each hit.

People ask me how I can retire at fifty-two. "You're still young. You have so much to give."

Yes, I am, and yes, I do, but I cannot do this forever. It's too painful.

It's one thing to have a child in front of me, flesh and blood

I can see and reach, but now, because of Celina, I must reach farther, farther than right here, right now, because her friend, her faceless, nameless friend, just might have a chance too.

And what if the girls in the group home start reading books? Will the group home people even notice?

Will one of them see what's inside these books?

Will they care?

Is it a Christian group home? Sinners to Saints Group Home? The Apostles for Jesus Group Home for Girls?

I realize again or maybe for the first time, I am book obsessed.

And now there will be one more person who knows, someone outside my fold, and it terrifies me.

The wrong person, the idle person, the person who does not spend 180 days of life dedicated to tiny strangers is going to call the school board, tell the world, "Words are wicked!" over and over until someone listens.

They'll pull me out of retirement and beat me down until I confess. "Yes, yes, I gave out porn. Is that what you want to hear? It's porn, pure porn!'

I see the protest signs, "Satan loves sex," and, "Labia don't belong in our libaries."

They will spell "libraries" incorrectly, of course.

Then a reader with panache for confirmation bias will attack me on social media with King James in his left hand and a cross in his right, and I will be done, my retirement days spent sharpening an endless supply of Office Depot pencils for the next benchmark test.

Celina is still smiling.

Doesn't she know the penis police are coming?

"Sweet. I hope she likes it," I say. "What am I saying? She'll like it."

"Yeah," she says.

This is it for me and Celina.

We hug, and she leaves.

I consider looking up her attendance to see how many days she came, but I won't. It doesn't matter. She came enough, enough to get one book inside her, enough for her to crave one more.

I really am the book pusher.

Take that, Celina Cantu. Defy me again, and I'll send a book to your house, make you read that too.

I have to laugh. I would do that.

As the final bell rings, Pacheco comes over the loud speaker reminding us to follow the students out to the sidewalk, all the wranglers and wrestlers telling all the wild horses to go on home for the last time.

Unlike Christmas, there's lots of hugging and squeezing, crying and consoling.

"Yes, you can find me on social media."

"Yes, you will always be able to find me on social media."

"I love you too."

I love you all. This has been a great time.

Really.

As if on cue, Jesus slithers by, the remaining serpent among the field of hooves.

"I heard you were retiring, Ms. Is that true?" he says.

I estimate I've been in contact with a few thousand children in my life. I have nothing to say to five of them.

"That's cool, that's cool," he says. "Well, good luck."

No need to bother with a proper thank-you when a blank stare will suffice. He walks away, seemingly unaware I never said a word.

Next to me Rodriguez sings, "School's out for summer."

Next to her Maggie sings, "You don't have to go home, but you can't stay here."

"Isn't that a song?" I say.

"Yep, but it applies here too," she says. "It will take me two months to recover from this year—the only child's face I want to see for the next two months is my own."

She doesn't mean it, but it is true.

I won't miss those conversations in the first month of school.

"You've never finished a book."

"Yes, I have."

"No, you haven't."

"Yes, I have."

"What have you read?"

"*Hatchet.*"

"That was with a teacher as a class."

"*Holes.*"

"That was with a teacher as a class."

"*Esperanza Rising.*"

"That was with a teacher as a class."

This would go on and on and on until they gave in to me, my power, my obsession.

"Okay, Ms. I haven't read a book. Can you help me?"

Aha! Then we could get started.

But not anymore.

I head to my room to grab my things. I consider getting weepy eyed, lamenting the years gone by, worrying about what will happen next, but it can all wait.

Right now the other district is calling my name.

ABOUT THE AUTHOR

Daphne Russell spent seventeen years in classroom settings as a middle-school reading teacher using class sets of *Hatchet* and *Esperanza Rising* until 2007 when a friend told her to read *The Book Thief* by Markus Zusak. She then began teaching as though books save lives, and has never wavered from that mission. As the designated Reading Specialist at Mansfeld Middle School, Russell was part of the faculty and staff who transformed their C rated school to an A+ school during the three years *Read or Die* was being written. s-She lives in Tucson, Arizona.